Two-Fer

Two-Fer

ELECTING A PRESIDENT AND A SUPREME COURT

CLINT BOLICK

HOOVER INSTITUTION PRESS

STANFORD UNIVERSITY | STANFORD, CALIFORNIA

www.hoover.org

Hoover Institution Press Publication No. 621

Hoover Institution at Leland Stanford Junior University,
Stanford, California 94305-6010

First printing 2012
18   17   16   15   14   13   12   7   6   5   4   3   2   1

Manufactured in the United States of America

The paper used in this publication meets the minimum
Requirements of the American National Standard for Information
Sciences—Permanence of Paper for Printed Library Materials,
ANSI/NISO Z39.48-1992. ∞

Cataloging-in-Publication Data is available from the
Library of Congress.
ISBN: 978-0-8179-1464-6 (cloth. : alk. paper)
ISBN: 978-0-8179-1466-0 (e-book)

For my friend George F. Will,
America's greatest political commentator,
with deep appreciation for his passion for freedom and baseball.

CONTENTS

ACKNOWLEDGMENTS

I AM VERY GRATEFUL to the Hoover Institution for publishing this book. As a constitutional litigator, I am reminded every day of the importance of the men and women who serve as judges on our federal and state courts—and of the people who appoint them. Although I am militantly independent in my politics, and rarely if ever have voted a straight party ticket, the fact is that political affiliation often matters greatly in the appointment of judges, which in turn sets the course of American law. In particular, when presidents name justices to the U.S. Supreme Court, they can be making the most significant decisions they ever make in terms of lasting and direct impact on the American people and their freedoms. Yet, while for those reasons the appointment of Supreme Court justices and other federal judges should be a central factor in choosing a president, judicial selection usually plays an invisible role in presidential campaigns. I hope this small book will help broaden the discourse about the importance of judicial nominations in current and future campaigns—not just in campaigns for president but also for the senators who confirm the nominees and the governors who appoint state court judges.

I am also grateful to the Goldwater Institute and its supporters for allowing me to engage in the enormously rewarding practice of constitutional law; and to my research assistants, Justin Bohall and Kathryn Blades, for their contributions to the book. To the reader, I offer my appreciation and the hope that you will find this book useful and provocative.

1

The Grand Prize

E VERY AMERICAN PRESIDENTIAL ELECTION presents
different burning issues. The Vietnam War dominated
three consecutive elections from 1964 to 1972. Scandals
from Teapot Dome to Watergate have figured prominently in
others. Recessions typically thrust economic issues to the fore-
front, leading one presidential campaign to adopt the famous
campaign imperative, "It's the economy, stupid!" Other issues
from abortion to forced busing to education to the environment
have made major appearances in national campaigns.

Issues come and go, and the impact of national elections in
resolving these issues sometimes is minor or fleeting. But one
issue that rarely makes even a cameo appearance in national
campaigns nonetheless may be the most important and enduring
consequence of electing a president: the party that controls the
White House also controls the appointment of the federal judiciary. This is one matter on which the party in power, especially

over the last several decades, makes a decided difference—which in turn directly affects the lives of every single American.

Judges typically operate in relative obscurity. Except for lawyers who practice before them, few Americans can name more than a few members of the U.S. Supreme Court, much less judges on other federal or state courts. Yet judges are powerful and important. Judges make decisions every day about religion, speech, property, business, education, civil rights, and myriad other issues that touch all of us in direct and immediate ways. They set the rules and guide the proceedings by which accused criminals are tried and punishment is meted out. Ultimately, they determine whether our most fundamental rights are enforced or destroyed.

Think for a moment about who the most powerful woman has been in American history. One might nominate several candidates, but unquestionably the most accurate answer is former United States Supreme Court Justice Sandra Day O'Connor. She served as an associate justice of the Supreme Court for a quarter century. Not only was she the first woman to serve on the Court, she was its only female member for most of her tenure. But for many years, she stood far taller in influence than her male colleagues, for typically she was the swing vote in many five-to-four decisions. On matters ranging from abortion to racial preferences to school vouchers to the rights of criminal defendants to federalism, hers was often the deciding vote, and that vote repeatedly changed the course of American history.

Nor is the U.S. Supreme Court necessarily more important than other federal courts. The Supreme Court accepts review in only a tiny fraction—sometimes as little as one percent—of the cases brought to it for review. The vast majority of federal cases are decided by the hundreds of judges who serve in federal district courts and courts of appeals.

And nor are federal courts in the aggregate necessarily the most important American courts. Most cases are brought in state courts. The vast majority of cases involving crimes, property, contracts, torts, and family law—often the most deeply personal types of cases—are decided in state courts. States have their own constitutions, which typically are more expansive and detailed than the U.S. Constitution. What is more—and as I will discuss in greater detail in the postscript—state courts are free to construe individual rights protected in their constitutions more broadly (but not more narrowly) than the rights protected by the federal Constitution.

So courts and judges are enormously important. And yet, come election time, almost nobody thinks about them. Why? Perhaps it is because we are taught in civics class that judges are insulated from politics. Federal judges, of course, have lifetime tenure and only can be removed through impeachment. Over the course of history, few have been removed. During their tenure, they enjoy an independence from political influence that most public officials only can dream about. This independence is a vital part of our republican system of government, for judges who are dependent upon the political branches of government (that is, the executive and legislative branches) are likely to be little inclined to hold those branches to the boundaries of their constitutional authority or to protect individual rights against government abuse.

But, in fact, federal courts are political institutions. Judges are appointed by the president, with the advice and consent of the

Senate. The appointment and confirmation of judges are enormously important powers precisely *because* judges are appointed for life. The Senate confirmation process in particular is important because it is the last democratic checkpoint before individuals are invested with enormous lifetime powers. Every American has a vital and direct interest in the appointment and confirmation of federal judges—which raises greatly the stakes in electing those individuals who have the power and responsibility to appoint and confirm them.

State courts and judges often are even more overtly political. The method of appointing and retaining judges varies widely among the states. In many states, judges are elected, with the result that judges owe their jobs to the electorate and, to varying degrees, to special-interest groups (often lawyers) who contribute to their campaigns. In other states, judges are appointed in a manner similar to the federal system. Still other states have a "merit selection" system in which an appointed body makes a limited number of recommendations for appointment to the governor. In such systems, the state bar often plays a significant role. Regardless of the method of initial appointment, many states have periodic retention elections for some or all of their judges.

The method of judicial selection may influence whether state judges are highly qualified professionals or political hacks. I have practiced in state courts from coast to coast and have found that, unlike the federal judiciary, the quality and integrity of state courts varies widely. In one Texas trial court in which I litigated a case, for instance, it was obvious that contributions to the judge's reelection campaign were expected—and everyone involved in the case, except me, appeared to have made one. In an Illinois case, the trial judge had served until recently as a state legislator, where he had opposed our position on the issue that was before the court. In a New York court, when I was litigating for the Institute for Justice, the court sent us mail addressed to the Institute for Injustice. It was no surprise when my colleagues and I lost all of those cases. And yet in other state courts, the quality and integrity of the judging was exceptional, with the outcome not at all appearing to have been preordained. So the appointment of state court judges is enormously important, even if it rarely appears on the radar screens of people and groups who are otherwise deeply involved in politics and public policy.

At the federal level, lifetime tenure for judges makes judicial appointments one of a president's most important and lasting legacies, for most of the judges will far outlast the administration that appointed them. President Ronald Reagan is four presidents removed from the present one, yet two of his appointees to the U.S. Supreme Court—Anthony Kennedy and Antonin Scalia— remain on the Court. Justice Scalia has been a leading conservative influence throughout his tenure, and Justice Kennedy is now the swing vote on the Court—so that Reagan continues to exert enormous ongoing influence over the nation's course more than 30 years after he was first elected and many years after his death.

At the same time, the current Supreme Court is precariously balanced along philosophical lines. The five conservative justices usually vote together in contested cases, and the four liberal justices almost always vote in lockstep. The liberal justices have exhibited little moderation except on business issues. Accordingly, the shift of a single justice could tilt the Court's balance sharply to the left—and if that happens, the liberal imbalance could remain that way for a generation, even if there were conservative presidents along the way.

This is because opportunities for presidents to nominate Supreme Court justices are rare, and opportunities to shift the Court's balance rarer still. Once a fairly solid conservative majority emerged on the Court in the 1990s, it survived eight years of the Bill Clinton presidency and, so far, three years of Barack Obama's presidency. Although both Clinton and Obama named justices, in each instance a liberal replaced a liberal. But, of course, the new justices were much younger than their predecessors, thus fortifying the liberal wing of the Court. The replacement of a single conservative justice by a younger liberal justice could lock a liberal majority into place for a long time. The replacement of older liberal justices with younger ones makes it much more difficult for a conservative president to influence the Court's direction. Similarly, the replacement of a liberal justice by a conservative one would cement the Court's conservative majority, and the replacement of older conservative justices with younger ones would strengthen it.

While appointments to the Supreme Court are increasingly rare, appointments to the lower federal courts are not, so that even if a president has no Supreme Court nominations at all, he or she still can deeply influence the course of the judiciary, especially given that the vast majority of federal cases are decided by district courts and courts of appeals. Recent presidents have named nearly one-quarter of all federal judges during each four-year term. Over two terms, President Reagan appointed 49 percent of the federal judiciary, while Bill Clinton named 43 percent over his eight years in office. Moreover, the number of federal judges often increases, giving the president at such times a special bounty of judicial appointments.

Two developments have increased the importance of Supreme Court nominations. First, nominations tend to be increasingly ideological. In days gone by, it was difficult to predict a justice's philosophy even if you knew his or her party affiliation. Some past presidents attempted to pack the Supreme Court for specific reasons. Abraham Lincoln, for instance, named justices who he believed would support his controversial Civil War measures. And after a bare majority of the Supreme Court repudiated some of his early New Deal ventures, Franklin Roosevelt famously proposed expanding the size of the Court so that he could shift the majority. Justice Owen Roberts's "switch in time that saved nine," in which he moved from New Deal opponent to supporter, rendered unnecessary Roosevelt's deeply unpopular threat. Still, even the justices appointed for particular purposes by those presidents were unpredictable and divided on other issues.

For instance, the *Slaughter-House Cases*[1] in 1873 presented a five-to-four Supreme Court split that was extremely rare in that era. The decision involved the privileges or immunities clause of the recently adopted Fourteenth Amendment. A group of butchers challenged a bribery-procured Louisiana slaughterhouse monopoly on the grounds that it violated their freedom of enterprise, whose protection was a principal goal of the Fourteenth Amendment's framers. A majority of the court, over three passionate dissenting opinions, ruled against the butchers, thereby obliterating the privileges or immunities clause and judicial protection for economic liberty.[2]

In *Slaughter-House*, the seven Republican justices divided four to three and the Democrats divided one apiece. More to the point, Lincoln's five appointees were split, with two joining the majority and three dissenting. It would be extremely unusual today to see that type of split in a contentious case among justices appointed by the same president.

Similarly, in the 1944 decision in *Korematsu v. United States*,[3] the infamous decision in which the U.S. Supreme Court upheld the internment of Japanese citizens, five justices appointed to the Court by Franklin Roosevelt (Hugo Black, Stanley Reed, William Douglas, Wiley Rutledge, and Felix Frankfurter) voted with the majority, while two others (Frank Murphy and Robert Jackson) dissented. (The two remaining justices appointed by Republican presidents split their votes.) While Roosevelt's appointees tended to align in support of New Deal issues, they were deeply divided over civil liberties.

Richard Nixon, who was elected in part due to popular reaction against the excesses of the Supreme Court under the leadership of Chief Justice Earl Warren, may have been the first president to make a concerted effort to name justices with broad, consistent judicial philosophies, specifically "strict constructionism." He failed.[4] Nowhere was that failure more apparent than in *Roe v. Wade*,[5] the 1973 decision establishing the right to abortion. By that time, Nixon had appointed four of the nine Supreme Court justices. Had all of them voted together, they could have formed a majority against the right to abortion. But three of the four (Harry Blackmun, Warren Burger, and Lewis Powell) voted in favor of the abortion right, while only one Nixon appointee, William Rehnquist, voted against. The two

Eisenhower holdovers, William Brennan Jr. and Potter Stewart, also voted in the majority; along with Thurgood Marshall, who was named to the Court by President Lyndon Johnson. The only justice joining Rehnquist in dissent was Byron White, a Democrat who was nominated to the Court by John F. Kennedy.

Throughout history, then, justices in landmark cases frequently departed from the philosophies of the presidents who appointed them, and a partisan divide on the Supreme Court was the exception rather than the rule.

That changed, starting with the election of President Reagan, who was far more systematic and successful than his predecessors in appointing judges and justices who shared his judicial philosophy. Since Reagan, Republican presidents have tended consistently to nominate conservative justices and judges, and Democrats have nominated liberal justices and judges with similar determination and success. In terms of the Supreme Court, the principal exception was Justice David Souter, nominated by the first President Bush, who was a consistently liberal vote. Even Justices Sandra Day O'Connor and Anthony Kennedy, who were appointed by Reagan and have occupied the Court's ideological center, have moved constitutional jurisprudence in a conservative direction. Democratic presidents since Reagan, though so far having had fewer appointments, have a perfect record in appointing justices with liberal philosophies. Put another way, neither party has made a "mistake" in Supreme Court appointments in more than two decades.

The ideological homogeneity of Supreme Court justices reflecting the philosophy of the presidents who appointed them is illustrated by numerous recent decisions. In both *McDonald v. Chicago*,[6] which applied the Second Amendment to the states to strike down Chicago's handgun ban, and *Citizens United v. Federal Elections Commission*,[7] in which the Court held that corporations have a protected First Amendment right to political speech, the Court was split five to four along now-familiar liberal and conservative lines. Among the liberal dissenters, only Justice John Paul Stevens was appointed by a Republican president. With his replacement by Justice Elena Kagan, who was appointed by President Barack Obama in 2010, there is perfect homogeneity within the Court's liberal and conservative wings, in that all five conservative justices were appointed by Republican presidents and all four liberals were appointed by Democrats.

That is not to say that the justices are partisan. Quite to the contrary, there are few cases in which the justices' partisan affiliations influence their decisions.[8] Rather, each of the justices have sincere, deeply held philosophical views on legal issues. Nor is that divide, much as some conservatives might simplistically wish to describe it, between judicial activism versus judicial restraint. Indeed, in recent years, some liberals have criticized conservative justices for being too activist, in the sense of striking down (in their view) too many laws. This is a charge I will discuss later, as I believe that the Court is not nearly activist enough in striking down unconstitutional laws.[9]

The divide between the Court's liberals and conservatives—and to some extent, the lesser divide within the two camps—emanates mainly from different views about the proper method by which to interpret the Constitution. The conservatives tend to advocate "original intent"—that is, an attempt to determine the original meaning of constitutional provisions and to apply them to contemporary circumstances. Even within that philosophy, there are variations, involving, for instance, placing different weight on constitutional text, the views of the framers, legislative history, and tradition. Some justices adhere strongly to the principle of *stare decisis*—that is, deference to precedents—while others do not. Some justices use foreign law to help interpret American law, while others disdain that practice. Among current justices, the leading advocate of judicial restraint—or, as he calls it, "judicial modesty"—is not a conservative but a liberal, Justice Breyer, who believes that courts should defer to manifestations of "active democracy."[10] In this regard he sounds more like the conservative legal scholar Robert Bork than like many of his liberal colleagues.

Still, despite some aberrations, especially in cases involving certain civil liberties, the five-to-four conservative/liberal split tends to hold on nearly all deeply contentious issues, ranging from racial preferences to religion to property rights. While much attention is focused on the cohesiveness of the Court's conservative majority—or at least the "core four" of Chief Justice Roberts and Justices Scalia, Thomas, and Alito—in fact, the four liberal justices (Justices Ginsburg, Breyer, Sonia Sotomayor, and Kagan) are even more cohesive. Every year the *New York Times* catalogues the votes of the justices for the prior Court Term. In the nine cases that the *Times* considered most important during the Court's 2010–11 Term, the four core conservatives voted in unison in six—while the liberals voted together in eight. Justice Thomas often is derided by liberals for voting so frequently with Justice Scalia—and indeed, he did so in 89 percent of the cases in 2010–11. But each pair among the liberal justices voted together between 85 and 94 percent of the time, exhibiting tremendous cohesion.

The deep philosophical divide on major issues between conservative and liberal Supreme Court justices underscores a very significant development in modern politics: the president's partisan affiliation makes a tremendous—indeed defining—difference in Supreme Court nominations. From a conservative or libertarian perspective, the worst Republican will be better than the best Democrat in terms of choosing judges; and the converse is equally true for liberals.

Why are judicial nominations more ideologically driven than ever before? And why have recent presidents proved more successful than their predecessors in appointing judges who reflect their judicial philosophies?

One explanation is the emergence of an organization that has done more to influence the selection of judges during Republican administrations than any other. The Federalist Society for Law and Policy Studies was formed in 1982[11] by law students at Harvard, Yale, and the University of Chicago, with support from former attorney general Edwin Meese, former solicitor general Theodore Olson, and former judge Robert Bork. The Federalist Society's mission was to counter the liberal influence in law schools, legal academia, and the practice of law. To say that it has succeeded in greatly advancing that mission over the past 30 years is a tremendous understatement.

From humble beginnings, the Federalist Society now has chapters at more than 200 law schools, with 10,000 law student members and 30,000 lawyer members. The group coheres around the principle that the proper role of judges is to determine what the law is, not what it should be. Apart from that core shared belief, a great deal of philosophical diversity exists within the predominantly conservative and libertarian ranks. For instance, Bork believes strongly that courts should almost always defer to the political branches and rarely if ever decide issues of public policy, while University of Chicago law professor Richard Epstein would have courts invalidate much state and federal legislation enacted over the past century—yet both are active Federalist Society boosters.

What the Federalist Society lacks in doctrinal dogma, it more than makes up for in the robust exchange of ideas. Nearly all of its activities consist of balanced debates on issues of legal philosophy. So important is that role that I have frequently heard liberal law school deans remark that if it were not for the Federalist Society, there would be no debates at all in their law schools.

By fostering such debate, the Federalist Society has given rise to legal academics and judges who have spent a great deal of time thinking about and developing judicial philosophies. Federalist Society members often in turn work as research assistants and law clerks to those professors and judges, and frequently go on to prestigious posts in legal academia, law practice, and the judiciary. All of that activity makes it easier for Republican presidents to nominate judges with well-developed philosophies who are unlikely to disappoint them after they join the bench.

The foment on the right has triggered a reaction on the left, including the creation of the American Constitution Society, which seeks to counter the Federalist Society's influence in law schools. (Happily, the two organizations often cosponsor debates, ensuring that the forums are well balanced and of high quality.)

As a result, both sides have a deep bench, pardon the pun, from which to draw for judicial appointments.

Augmenting the increased supply of potential judges whose philosophies of law are fairly well known in advance is the recognition among both Republican and Democratic presidents that judicial nominees are very important to their respective political bases. Whatever their perceived apostasies on public policy issues, presidents can mollify their core constituencies when they appoint judges to their liking. Or at the very least, they have learned not to name judges who alienate their core constituencies. A case in point was President George W. Bush's nomination of White House counsel Harriet Miers to the Supreme Court. Though Miers may have been conservative, her views were not sufficiently well known nor her philosophical bona fides established enough to satisfy movement conservatives. The resulting tempest brought down the nomination and resulted in the appointment of Justice Samuel Alito, Jr., a superb choice from a conservative perspective.

The second development that has increased the importance of judicial nominations is human longevity. It is often remarked that if people want to live a long life, they should become Supreme Court justices; if they want to live a short life, they should become retired Supreme Court justices. The few individuals who serve on the nation's highest court typically stay until a very advanced age. Justice Thurgood Marshall once remarked, when asked about the possibility of retirement, that he had a lifetime appointment and intended to serve every day of it.

Lifetime tenure is far more meaningful than it was when the Constitution was ratified. Life expectancy today is roughly double what it was in the late 1700s. Naming someone to a lifetime post was not that big a deal when, as in the late eighteenth century, the average age of the nominees was 50 and average life expectancy was in the 30s. It is a much bigger deal in the twenty-first century, in which the average age at appointment to the Supreme Court is about 52 and average life expectancy is 76. To take the most recent example, when Justice Elena Kagan was nominated at age 50, her total life expectancy was 85 years. Hence, assuming good health and a desire to serve out her term, Justice Kagan's expected tenure would be 35 years—spanning nearly nine presidential terms. That is a serious presidential legacy.

The average age at which justices are nominated to the Supreme Court has not changed significantly since our nation's early days. In the first 25 years following the Constitution, the average age of Supreme Court nominees was 50; today it is about 52. The average age of nominees increased to nearly 59 in the latter part of the nineteenth century and the first half of the twentieth century. But modern presidents seem to be catching on to the prospect of a lasting legacy: since 1972, only one of the dozen confirmed justices had a six in the first digit of her age (Ruth Bader Ginsburg, nominated at age 60). All of the remainder were in their 50s, except for Clarence Thomas, who brought down the average by having been named to the Court at age 43. If he serves to the same age as his predecessor, Thurgood Marshall (age 83), he will be on the Court for 40 years—and despite having been appointed by the elder President Bush in 1991, he is only midway through that tenure. If he serves that long, he will eclipse the record tenure of Justice William Douglas, who served on the Court for 36 years.

Figure 1. Average Age of Justices When Appointed and Life Expectancy of the Time Period

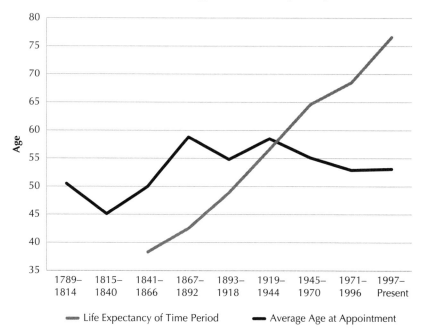

Figure 1 illustrates the average age of justices at the time of appointment, compared with the expected life expectancy at birth during the same period.

The figure illustrates that while the age at appointment has remained relatively constant, life expectancy has increased dramatically. This in turn has led to a marked increase in the average tenure of Supreme Court justices, which has grown from 8 years at the beginning of the republic to 24½ years today, as depicted in Figure 2.

Hence, lifetime tenure for Supreme Court justices has become an enormous prize for presidents whose importance continues to

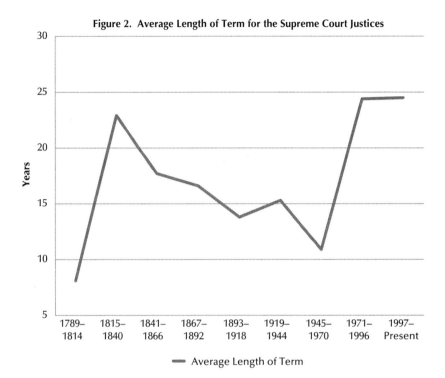

Figure 2. Average Length of Term for the Supreme Court Justices

grow—and both sides of the ideological divide are keenly aware of the stakes.

Those stakes have translated into bitter Supreme Court confirmation battles—but only when control of the Court is at stake. Republicans generally have been content to allow relatively smooth confirmation of liberal justices who replace other liberals, and vice versa. But the two most recent nominations that affected the Court's balance evoked vicious confirmation battles.

The first was the nomination of Robert Bork to succeed Justice Lewis Powell, Jr., who occupied the center of the Court toward the end of his tenure. Bork would have fortified the conservative wing and moved the Court solidly to the right. Led by Senator Edward Kennedy, Democrats strongly opposed the nomination, in some instances exaggerating Bork's views. Bork defended himself gamely but to no avail—his nomination was defeated. President Reagan then nominated Judge Douglas Ginsburg, a libertarian whose nomination was withdrawn because, as a law professor, Ginsburg had smoked marijuana with students. Having failed twice, Reagan turned to Judge Anthony Kennedy, a noncontroversial conservative.

The fallout from the Bork nomination led to the 1990 nomination of Judge David Souter, who had served as a justice on the New Hampshire Supreme Court and a judge on the U.S. Court of Appeals for the First Circuit without a clear philosophical record. Democrats suspected that Souter was a "stealth" nominee—and President Bush no doubt intended him to be one—but Souter turned out to be a solid liberal vote on the Supreme Court. An important lesson was learned, and subsequent presidents have taken great pains—with great success—to satisfy themselves that their Supreme Court nominees will not disappoint them.

Following Souter came the political cataclysm over the nomination of Judge Clarence Thomas, which would replace the Court's most liberal justice (Thurgood Marshall) with arguably its most conservative. Liberals were not about to let that happen without a nasty fight in which no means was beyond consideration to achieve the desired ends. Opponents searched Thomas's trash cans and scoured the country for anyone who could damage the nominee. In the end, Thomas prevailed by a 52-to-48 vote in the Senate. But the battle against the nomination marked a new low in political discourse, which we are all too likely to see again the next time a nominee might alter the present balance on the Supreme Court.

Although Supreme Court nominations since Thomas have been relatively quiet affairs because they have not altered the Court's ideological balance, there have been numerous confirmation battles over lower-court nominations, especially where confirmation might help credential the nominees for future vacancies on the U.S. Supreme Court. In 2001, President George W. Bush nominated an exceptionally bright conservative, Miguel Estrada, to the U.S. Court of Appeals for the District of Columbia Circuit—a court from which many Supreme Court justices are nominated. Estrada immigrated to the United States from Honduras and could have been the first Hispanic justice in a future Republican administration. Democrats successfully filibustered the nomination and Estrada never made it to the court.

Republicans returned the favor when President Obama in 2010 nominated Berkeley law professor Goodwin Liu to the Ninth Circuit. A liberal who had written several provocative publications and had testified against the confirmation of Justice Alito, Liu would have been positioned to be the first Asian-American appointee to the Supreme Court in a future Democratic administration. Unable to win a cloture vote on the nomination, Liu withdrew his nomination.

Sometimes opposition to federal court nominees backfires. In the case of Goodwin Liu, following the withdrawal of his Ninth Circuit nomination, he was appointed by Governor Jerry Brown to the California Supreme Court, where he is likely to have great influence in the development of state constitutional law and develop strong credentials for future consideration as a nominee to the U.S. Supreme Court. But perhaps the most ironic twist of fate was the Senate's rejection in 1986 of Jefferson Sessions's nomination to serve as a judge on the federal district court in Alabama. He might have toiled in relative obscurity in that position. Instead, 10 years after the Senate torpedoed his judicial nomination, Sessions was elected to the U.S. Senate and was appointed to the Judiciary Committee, where he—you guessed it—sits in judgment on judicial nominees. When it comes to nominations made by Democratic presidents, Sessions often proves to be a tough sell.

Given the huge and central importance of federal judicial nominations, it is striking that the issue rarely comes up in presidential contests. Occasionally it does. Certainly the Warren Court played a significant role in the 1968 election of Richard Nixon, especially as part of his strategy to break the Democrats' control over the South. Similarly, Democrats sometimes have raised the specter of a conservative Court overturning *Roe v. Wade* and the right to abortion. Ironically, when it appeared that the Court might overturn *Roe*, it was three Republican appointees—Sandra Day O'Connor, Anthony Kennedy, and David Souter—who provided the crucial votes to preserve the right to abortion and arguably to place it on stronger jurisprudential ground.[12] Since then, however, judicial appointments have not been a galvanizing electoral issue for liberals or conservatives.

This is strange given the important issues that have been and are coming before the Court. Certainly since the early days of the New Deal, there has not been a Supreme Court whose philosophical compass is as opposed to that of a presidential administration as the current Court is in juxtaposition to the Obama administration. And yet the Court's five-to-four conservative majority hangs in precarious balance.

As this book goes to press in early 2012, four of the current justices, two conservatives (Scalia and Kennedy, both age 75) and two liberals (Ginsburg, 78, and Breyer, 73)—are in their 70s. The odds are great that one of our next presidents will have the first opportunity in over two decades to alter the Court's ideological balance, either fortifying the conservative majority or tilting it to a liberal majority. Either way, this will determine in large measure the future course of our nation. The opportunity to alter the Court's five-to-four balance has not occurred in over two decades, since Clarence Thomas replaced Thurgood Marshall. Since then, there have been six Supreme Court appointments—but they were four liberals replacing liberals and two conservatives replacing conservatives. To be sure, the nominations made the respective wings of the Court younger, and, in the case of Justice Alito replacing Justice O'Connor, strengthened the Court's conservative majority. But the five-to-four conservative majority now is beginning its third decade. Whether it will endure or be changed depends on whom Americans elect as president in the next election or two.

And yet, despite stakes that could hardly be greater, judicial nominations have not emerged as a coherent campaign issue in the 2012 contest. When the issue arises, usually it takes the form of judge-bashing. In the 2012 primaries, for instance, former house speaker Newt Gingrich advocated hauling judges before Congress to explain their thinking in court decisions and urged abolishing courts with which conservatives disagree—citing with approval, oddly enough, the example of President Franklin D. Roosevelt's efforts to bend the judiciary to his will. Texas governor Rick Perry urges doing away with lifetime tenure for federal judges, which of course would require a constitutional amendment. He failed to note the irony that the longest-serving justices—and hence the first to be replaced under a regime of term limits—are the justices with whom he tends to strongly agree.

What such proposals overlook is that the framers of the Constitution created a remedy for federal judges that the people do not like: electing a president who will appoint better ones. As the next chapter demonstrates, there were very good reasons for the framers to fashion the judiciary the way they did. And there would be grave costs to freedom if we decided to tinker with or distort that design.

The bottom line is that for presidents fortunate enough to have the opportunity to do so, the nomination of Supreme Court justices is probably the most important and enduring decision they will ever make. Appointments to lower federal courts, which every president makes in abundance, also are enormously significant.

Hence, in a very real sense, the power to nominate federal judges is the grand prize in presidential elections. Deciding who will wield that power provides perhaps the most compelling reason to vote either for a Republican or Democrat for president. For in the realm of judicial appointments—far more than in foreign policy, economic policy, and even social policy—the president's party affiliation will make an enormous difference. A Republican president may disappoint his or her base by creating a massive new entitlement program or declaring that it is necessary to destroy capitalism in order to save it. A Democratic president may disappoint the base by engaging in foreign wars or declaring that some businesses are too big to fail. But recent experience suggests that they will rarely if ever disappoint their respective core supporters on judicial nominations. And the nominations they make will have tangible consequences for generations to come.

2

The Framers' Vision

I N THE VIEW of many on both right and left, courts today are out of control. Both liberals and conservatives complain when courts strike down laws that they like. After all, the laws were enacted through the democratic process. Many on both sides of the ideological divide agree with the notion that courts should defer to majoritarian will. But both sides also tend to criticize courts for upholding laws that they do not like in addition to wanting them to sustain laws that they do. Adding to the confusion is the way critics often accuse the courts of "judicial activism" regardless of whether they are upholding or striking down laws. Some critics, however, are very consistent in their belief that judges always or nearly always should yield to popular will. Robert Bork, for example, has suggested that judicial review of the constitutionality of laws might properly be eliminated altogether.

For some who are fed up with the courts, that suggestion may at first blush appear tantalizing. But consider that possibility for a moment: a nation in which laws, no matter how outrageous or excessive or oppressive, could not be challenged in court. We would be forced to rely on the willingness of elected (and appointed) government officials to abide by constitutional limits on their authority and not to violate individual rights—certainly not a bet I would take. Such a situation would render worthless the written guarantees of our constitutions and would make America resemble third-world regimes that have little regard for the rule of law and the sanctity of individual rights. No matter how frustrating court decisions sometimes may be, this frustration pales in comparison to what our nation would be like if courts were divested of the power to determine the constitutionality of laws.

But what if this were what the framers of the U.S. Constitution intended? After all, many of the judiciary's fiercest critics consider themselves adherents to the doctrine of original constitutional intent. Did the framers envision a judiciary that deferred to majority rule, as expressed through elected representatives? Or did they intend the courts to provide an effective check on the excesses of the executive and legislative branches by negating laws that exceed their assigned powers?

The answer to this set of questions lies in the framers' decision to create not a democracy but a constitutional republic. In this system, the framers intended the judiciary to play a very robust role in curbing abuses of government power and protecting individual rights.[1]

The framers based their construction of the proper role of the judiciary upon two key insights that are even more salient in our day than in theirs.

The first, articulated in *The Federalist No. 10*, was the recognition that "factions," or what we today call special-interest groups, tend to manipulate the power of government to their own ends. As government has proliferated and grown ever more powerful, this insight has grown even more important. Not only does government regulate all manner of activities that were not even remotely contemplated at our nation's founding, thus raising the stakes for special-interest groups to manipulate government powers to their own benefit, but these powers increasingly are exercised by unelected agencies and officials that are not directly accountable to government powers.

The framers devised numerous mechanisms to check the abuse of power by factions: federalism, separation of powers, an express enumeration of federal government powers, guarantees of individual rights—and an independent judiciary. This was the framers' second key insight, set forth in *The Federalist No. 78*: that only through an independent judiciary could the other branches of government effectively be held to their assigned and limited authority. The constitutional mechanisms designed to limit government power and protect individual rights would not be worth the paper on which they were written if there were no authority that could protect them. This vital role was assigned to the courts.

The framers recognized that one of the principal threats to freedom was the people themselves. "Wherever the real power in a Government lies, there is the danger of oppression," Madison warned in a letter to Thomas Jefferson. In the United States, "the real power lies in the majority of the Community," Madison explained, "and the invasion of private rights is chiefly to be apprehended, not from acts of Government contrary to the sense of its constituents, but from acts in which Government is the mere instrument of the major number of its constituents."[2] The recognition that the majority could wield power in unjust ways was a major motivation for the enactment of the Bill of Rights, which made clear that certain rights—including unenumerated rights—could not be infringed no matter how large or powerful the majority backing the infringement.

Especially invidious to Madison was the evil of faction, which Madison defined in *The Federalist No. 10* as "a number of citizens, whether amounting to a majority or minority of the whole, who are united and actuated by some common impulse of passion, or of interest, adverse to the rights of other citizens, or to the permanent and aggregate interests of the community." Madison understood that the "latent causes of faction are . . . sown into the nature of man." All of history is replete with examples of despots or combinations of individuals seeking to manipulate the power of government for their own ends, to the detriment of others.

Madison postulated that there were only two ways to control the evil of factions: either to deprive them of their liberty to operate or to control their effects. As to the first option, observed Madison, "it could never be more truly said . . . that it was worse than the disease." What comes to mind from Madison's commentary is the spectacle of campaign finance laws, one piled on top of the other, which infringe upon the free-speech rights of political speakers while doing little to curb the influence of powerful interests in government.

Rather, the proper course, Madison insisted, was that factions "must be rendered . . . unable to concert and carry into effect schemes of oppression." To this end were a number of constitutional mechanisms directed, including the Bill of Rights and, later, the guarantee of equal protection under law.

One course that would not prove fruitful, Madison urged, was to allow elected officials to judge the limits of their own constitutional authority. He cited examples of tariffs and laws governing the obligations of debtors, whose constitutionality in the absence of checks on democracy would be determined solely by whichever side had greater influence. "Justice ought to hold the balance between them," Madison declared, yet "it is vain to say that enlightened statesmen will be able to adjust these clashing interests, and render them all subservient to the public good." In this observation, Madison would be proven clairvoyant time and again.

In addition to the limits on government power and protections of individual rights contained in the Constitution, there needed to be an objective arbiter that could interpret these provisions and protect the common good rather than special interests. Fortunately, the framers had experience with the benefits of an independent judiciary. In English common law, although courts could not invalidate acts of Parliament, they could strike down actions of the Crown and of local governments. Similarly, in several states, courts invoked power under their constitutions to invalidate laws. During the Constitution's ratification, the judiciary's power to invalidate unconstitutional laws was widely acknowledged by both supporters and opponents.

During the ratification debate, in an effort to assure state legislatures that the powers conferred upon the national government by the new Constitution would be effectively limited, Alexander Hamilton sketched out the vital role of an independent judiciary in *The Federalist No. 78*. Drawing upon the role of the judiciary in

England, Hamilton observed that in "a monarchy it is an excellent barrier to the despotism of the prince; in a republic it is a no less excellent barrier to the encroachments and concessions of the representative body." Accordingly, he argued, "the courts of justice are to be considered as the bulwarks of a limited Constitution against legislative encroachments." Specifically, they were "designed to be an intermediate body between the people and the legislature, in order . . . to keep the latter within the limits assigned to their authority." Speaking to the concerns about faction raised by Madison, Hamilton declared that courts would guard against "dangerous innovations in the government, and serious oppressions of the minor party in the community."

The mechanism by which the judiciary would dispatch this critical responsibility would become known as "judicial review." The Constitution, Hamilton asserted, obliged the courts "to declare all acts contrary to the manifest tenor of the Constitution void. Without this, all the reservations of particular rights or privileges amount to nothing." Hamilton's argument in favor of judicial review is so persuasive that it is worth quoting at length:

> No legislative act . . . contrary to the Constitution, can be valid. To deny this, would be to affirm, that the deputy is greater than his principal; that the servant is above his master; that the representatives of the people are superior to the people themselves; that men acting by virtue of their powers, may do not only what their powers do not authorize, but what they forbid. . . . Nor does this conclusion by any means suppose a superiority of the judicial to the legislative authority. It only supposes that the power of the people is superior to both; and that where the will of the legislature,

declared in its statutes, stands in opposition to that of the people, declared in the Constitution, the judges ought to be governed by the latter rather than the former. They ought to regulate their decisions by the fundamental laws, rather than by those which are not fundamental.

The role of judicial review is vitally important and is what vexes conservative and liberal critics alike. But when such critics condemn the actions of courts in striking down unconstitutional laws, it is important to recognize that their quarrel is not with the courts but with the framers, who understood that judicial review was essential in ensuring that the Constitution would reign supreme over majoritarian impulses or special-interest pressures.

Hamilton asserted in *No. 78* that among the three branches of government, the judiciary would be the "least dangerous to the political rights of the Constitution; because it will be least in a capacity to annoy or injure them." That is because while the executive and legislative branches enjoy affirmative powers, the courts "may truly be said to have neither FORCE nor will, but merely judgment." In other words, while the executive and legislative branches could seek to push the boundaries of their powers in ways that invaded constitutional rights, the courts can exercise their muscle only by restricting the powers of the other two branches.

But Hamilton recognized that in certain circumstances the judiciary could endanger freedom. Although "liberty can have nothing to fear from the judiciary alone," it "would have every thing to fear from its union with either of the other departments."

As a consequence, Hamilton warned, the judiciary must remain "truly distinct from both the legislature and the Executive."

That insight defines the crucial difference between legitimate judicial review and illegitimate judicial lawmaking. It is not improper for the courts to strike down unconstitutional laws; indeed, that is their vital role in limiting the excesses of the other two branches and protecting individual rights. Where courts get themselves into trouble—and stray beyond legitimate judicial activism into improper and dangerous judicial lawlessness—is where they exercise executive or legislative powers.

Modern examples abound. For instance, when courts take over the administration of schools or prisons, they are exercising executive powers. When they impose taxes or funding obligations, or when they create new laws (such as the "Miranda rule" for informing criminal defendants of their rights, or the trimester rule in the abortion context, or the imposition of forced busing or racial quotas), they are exercising legislative powers. When they do so, they become truly dangerous, in large measure because, unlike the exercise of such powers by the legislative or executive branches, it is difficult or impossible to correct those excesses through democratic processes. This type of judicial excess was rampant in the courts during the period in which Chief Justice Earl Warren presided over the U.S. Supreme Court, and it led to intense and well-deserved public criticism of the courts.

Courts sometimes also veer from the framers' intent in another important way: when they *fail* to enforce constitutional constraints on the powers of the other branches or protections of individual rights. In this sense, the judiciary properly can be accused of insufficient activism. Courts abdicate their core function of judicial review in two distinct ways.

First, they create artificial barriers to challenging unconstitutional government actions. Again, examples are numerous. For instance, taxpayers are deemed not to have standing in federal courts to challenge constitutional violations. In order to have standing to sue, a person must have sustained a direct and tangible injury, different from other members of the community— with the perverse consequence that the more widely inflicted the constitutional injury, the less likely that it can be challenged in court. Similarly, federal courts apply a "presumption of constitutionality" to most government actions, as opposed to the skepticism that should accompany actions that appear to press constitutional boundaries or impact individual rights.[3] Some issues, such as the making of war, are deemed "political questions" whose resolution is entrusted entirely to the legislative and executive branches, even though the Constitution expressly limits and separates their respective roles and powers. As a result of such judicially created obstacles, in many instances there is literally no one who can go to court to enforce the Constitution— which means we must rely entirely on the good faith of the executive and legislative branches, without the intervention of an independent, disinterested judicial referee—and to raise questions whose resolution in some instances could determine the future and very existence of our constitutional republic.

Second, in many instances, as I will describe in greater detail in the next section, courts have refused to meaningfully enforce constitutional provisions at all, such as the Ninth Amendment, which protects rights that are not expressly enumerated in the Constitution; the Contract Clause, which forbids the impairment of the obligation of contract; and the Fourteenth Amendment, which prevents state infringement of the privileges or immunities of citizens. In other cases, the Supreme Court essentially has amended constitutional provisions, such as by expanding the power of eminent domain under the Fifth Amendment to encompass not only the taking of property for public "use" but also the taking of anything that provides a public "benefit" and by expanding the narrow congressional power to regulate interstate commerce to encompass virtually any human activity (or even inactivity).

In such cases, the courts abdicate their critical roles in holding the elected branches to their assigned powers and protecting individual rights. Such judicial abdication does grave damage to our constitutional republic and to the individual liberties it is intended to safeguard. When courts fail to enforce the Constitution, typically they say that the proper recourse is through democratic processes—which offers hollow comfort given that presumably it was democratic processes that created the constitutional violation in the first place. In such instances, if the courts fail to enforce the Constitution, the Constitution will not be enforced at all.

Yet for all of the instances in which courts have exceeded their own constitutional boundaries or failed to enforce constitutional guarantees, there are countless examples of courts coming to the rescue of precious constitutional protections. It was one such case, *Brown v. Board of Education*,[4] in which the Supreme Court struck down the pernicious widespread practice of subjugating an entire race through "separate but equal" laws, that inspired me (and no doubt many others) to pursue a career in law. Absent judicial action to check the power of government and protect individual rights, government at every level would run roughshod over our liberties.

In the next two chapters, I will review briefly the uneven history of the federal courts in fulfilling the crucial role intended for them by our Constitution's framers and assess the generally exemplary record of the current Supreme Court in vindicating the framers' vision. For better or worse, the courts will exert a tremendous real-world impact regardless of whether they fulfill or betray their central role as guardians of constitutional boundaries and rights. This is why it is so important to very carefully consider who will possess the awesome power to nominate and confirm judges.

3

The First Two Centuries

AN UNEVEN JUDICIAL RECORD

I T TOOK MORE THAN a dozen years for the Supreme Court to begin to play the important role intended by the framers. In its first years, the Court was relegated to a small room in the unfinished Capitol, which also was used for church services on Sunday (imagine what the American Civil Liberties Union would think of that today!). The Court rarely met and decided no cases of constitutional consequence. The principal function of the individual justices was to "ride circuit" and decide cases in the hinterlands.

That role began to change when, late in his term, President John Adams appointed as chief justice his secretary of state, John Marshall, a partisan Federalist from Virginia who was both Thomas Jefferson's cousin and political opponent. In what would be considered a grave conflict today, Marshall continued to serve as secretary of state. When the Republicans won the presidential election and control of Congress, Adams made a number of "midnight" judgeship appointments on the last night of his presidency.

Ironically, given that his actions would come before the Court in its first landmark decision, Marshall was responsible as secretary of state for delivering the hastily approved commissions. Some of the commissions were never delivered, and, after Thomas Jefferson was sworn in as president, they disappeared altogether.

Among them was a justice of the peace commission that had been approved by Congress and signed by Marshall for William Marbury, a Federalist from Maryland.[1] After failing to persuade Jefferson's secretary of state, James Madison, to deliver the commission, Marbury asked the Supreme Court to order Madison to do so.

Marbury's case presented the highly controversial question of whether the Supreme Court possessed the power to invalidate unconstitutional acts by the other branches of the federal government or to order them to conform to the law. Despite all historical evidence to the contrary, Republicans argued that the executive and legislative branches were vested with the power to determine the constitutionality of their own actions. Given that Republicans controlled all of the levers of government except the courts, a decision ordering Madison to deliver the commissions could have sparked a constitutional crisis, with the Jefferson administration likely to defy the order and possibly render the Court impotent. But if the Court backed down, it would have the same effect.

Sacrificing short-term political advantage for the long-term objective of establishing the power of the judiciary to determine constitutionality, Marshall adroitly navigated the political maelstrom in a brilliant decision.[2] The Court found that Marbury was in fact legally entitled to the commission. However, Marshall ruled that Congress had exceeded its authority under the Constitution by expanding the jurisdiction of the Court through the Judiciary Act of 1789. Because the Judiciary Act was the source of the Court's authority to order the president to deliver the disputed commission, the Court found that the act was unconstitutional, and therefore the Court could not order Madison to deliver the commission.

Though legally shaky on multiple grounds, the decision was a tour de force, accomplishing three outcomes at once: (1) it established the Court's authority to determine whether the executive branch was properly enforcing the law; (2) it established the Court's authority to declare acts of Congress unconstitutional; and (3) it avoided a constitutional crisis by finding that it could not order the requested relief. Hence, Madison nominally won the case, but Marshall unquestionably won the war. William Marbury never served as justice of the peace, but Chief Justice Marshall firmly and forever established the principle of judicial review in American law.

In asserting the judicial power to strike down unconstitutional laws, Marshall echoed Alexander Hamilton's exposition of the role of the judiciary set forth in *The Federalist No. 78*. The Constitution, he argued, "is either a superior, paramount law, unchangeable by ordinary means, or it is on a level with ordinary legislative acts, and like other acts, is alterable when the legislature shall please to alter it." If the latter is true, he continued, "then written constitutions are absurd attempts, on the part of the people, to limit a power, in its own nature illimitable." The consequence "would be giving to the legislature a practical and real omnipotence," even as the Constitution "professes to restrict [its] powers within narrow limits." The Court rejected that view, declaring that "an act of the legislature, repugnant to the constitution, is void" and that "[i]t is emphatically the province and the duty of the judiciary to say what the law is."

Marbury v. Madison is a milestone in the development of republican government and the American rule of law. Judicial review is a major distinction between free and totalitarian countries. Lots of countries have constitutions, but far fewer have independent judiciaries that can and do enforce the constitutions to prevent government despotism. Freedom advocates should cheer, not disdain, this feature of American republicanism, even if the courts in specific cases do not always please us.

And indeed, the courts' role in enforcing the constitution has been uneven. Americans who expected the judiciary in the wake of *Marbury v. Madison* to play an active role in protecting liberty would have to wait for nearly a century. Before the Civil War, the U.S. Supreme Court did not issue many sweeping opinions; and when it did, generally it declined to strike down laws. In its 1833 decision in *Barron v. Mayor and City Council of Baltimore*,[3] for instance, the Court ruled that the Fifth Amendment—which protects due process and limits the power of eminent domain—did not, despite its broad language, apply to local governments, so that, while the Bill of Rights restricted the power of the national government, it did not protect individuals against state or local government abuses.

The most infamous decision of the era and a paramount example of the judiciary's abdication of its core constitutional role was *Dred Scott v. Sandford* in 1853.[4] The plaintiff was an emancipated black who attempted to invoke the jurisdiction of the courts to file a lawsuit. The question framed by the Court was whether "a negro [can] become a member of the political community formed and brought into existence by the Constitution . . . and as such become entitled to all the rights . . . guaranteed by that instrument to the citizen." Apart from recognizing the institution of human slavery, the original Constitution did not draw any distinction between whites and blacks (or, for that matter, men and women). Nonetheless, in a brazen act of judicial lawlessness, the Court resorted not to the words of the Constitution but to the practices of those who created it. At that time, the Court observed, blacks were "considered as a subordinate and inferior class of beings, who had been dominated by the dominant race, and whether emancipated or not, yet remained subject to their authority, and had no rights or privileges but such as those who held the power and the government might choose to grant them." Dred Scott was turned away from the Court empty handed.

The notorious *Dred Scott* ruling was very much on the minds of those who waged political campaigns leading up to the Civil War. Abraham Lincoln, in particular, repudiated the notion that blacks were excluded from the principles of the Declaration of Independence and the protection of the Constitution. Among those joining the newly formed Republican Party, there also was a growing recognition that state governments, which in the original constitutional scheme were expected to be reliable guardians of liberty, too often instead were a source of oppression.

As a consequence, a period of profound constitutional transformation occurred in the aftermath of the Civil War. The radical

Republicans who pushed through constitutional change were not rebelling against the principles of the original Constitution. To the contrary, they embraced passionately the natural-rights philosophy that animated the Constitution. But having learned from the lessons of history, they concluded that, in light of those principles, the original Constitution was a flawed and unfinished document.

First, of course, came the Thirteenth Amendment, which abolished slavery. Later, came the Fifteenth Amendment, which guaranteed the most essential political right, the right to vote.

But perhaps the most important concern addressed by the Reconstruction Congress was to prevent states from ever again subjugating their citizens. Those efforts were made urgent by ongoing deprivations of important rights. Beaten but not chastened, recalcitrant Southern states were determined to reestablish the reality if not the formal condition of slavery through laws called the "black codes." These laws were designed to negate the most basic and essential civil rights of blacks, which were necessary for their true emancipation: freedom of contract, freedom of enterprise, and private property rights.[5]

Initially, Congress voted to protect those rights in the Civil Rights Act of 1866. But proponents feared that Congress lacked the constitutional authority to enact civil rights protections, and President Andrew Johnson vetoed it on that basis.[6] Thereafter, Congress determined to "constitutionalize" the protections of the Civil Rights Act. They proposed the Fourteenth Amendment, whose first section contained three essential protections: that state governments shall not "make or enforce any law which shall abridge the privileges or immunities of citizens of the

United States" (the privileges or immunities clause); that they may not "deprive any person of life, liberty, or property, without due process of law" (the due process clause); and that they shall not deny to any person within their jurisdictions "the equal protection of the laws" (the equal protection clause).

The Fourteenth Amendment's due process clause essentially overturned the *Barron* decision, extending the guarantee of due process to state governments. The equal protection clause safeguarded individuals against special-interest legislation that might be imposed upon them by their states.

But it was the Fourteenth Amendment's first protection—the privileges or immunities clause—that was designed to protect substantive rights against state governments. "Privileges and immunities" was a widely recognized term at the time, understood to encompass basic civil rights (such as those expressly guaranteed by the Bill of Rights) and other rights that belonged to all free people, such as freedom of contract, private property rights, and freedom of enterprise—the rights that Congress had attempted to protect in the Civil Rights Act of 1866.

Had the courts vigorously enforced the privileges or immunities clause—as they generally have fairly vigorously enforced the due process and equal protection guarantees—our nation would be a very different place today. Protection of freedom of enterprise would be as strongly protected as such other important rights as freedom of speech and religion.

But the reality is that government at every level today runs roughshod over freedom of enterprise, with the bizarre effect that the "right" to a welfare check receives greater judicial protection (under the due process clause) than the right to earn an honest living. Government can regulate businesses and professions with impunity, even if its aim is economic protectionism.

This perverse state of affairs traces to one of the most profound examples of judicial abdication in American history: the *Slaughter-House Cases* in 1873.[7] There the U.S. Supreme Court, by a five-to-four decision (a split that is common today but was exceedingly rare in the nineteenth century), narrowly construed the privileges or immunities clause only to protect a handful of rights of "national citizenship" that were expressly protected in the original Constitution, such as the right of access to ports and navigable waters and the right to travel from state to state and enjoy the same rights as other state's citizens. As for other rights, citizens would have to rely on state courts to protect them—cold comfort considering that by definition it was the states in such cases that were violating the rights in the first place.

The *Slaughter-House* dissenters were astounded that a civil war had been fought with no greater gain for the protection of rights than that. Justice Noah Swayne argued that to the contrary, the Fourteenth Amendment was intended "to rise to the dignity of a new Magna Charta." Instead, as another dissenter, Justice Stephen Field, declared that by the Court's decision essentially repealing the privileges or immunities clause, "the right of free labor, one of the most sacred and imprescriptable rights of man, is violated."

Indeed, just after *Slaughter-House*, the Court ruled in *Bradwell v. State*[8] that Illinois permissibly could exclude women from the practice of law. Rather than applying the law in a neutral and objective fashion, the Court engaged in classic judicial legislation. "Man is, or should be, woman's protector and defender," declared Justice Joseph Bradley in a dissenting opinion. "The natural and proper timidity and delicacy which belongs to the female sex evidently unfits it for many of the occupations of civil life," he asserted. The "paramount destiny and mission of woman," Bradley concluded, "are to fulfill the noble and benign offices of wife and mother."

The Court's wrecking-ball approach to the Fourteenth Amendment did not stop there. In *U.S. v. Cruikshank*[9] in 1875, the Court ruled that the privileges or immunities clause did not protect the Second Amendment right to keep and bear arms, thus extinguishing for a time the hope that the courts would apply the Bill of Rights to the states. Indeed, the Second Amendment would not be applied to the states for more than a century.

The case emanated from a brutal incident in 1873 called the Colfax Massacre, in which a group of armed white men murdered as many as 165 mainly unarmed black men. Although 97 assailants were indicted, only 3 were convicted—not of murder but of violating the federal Enforcement Act of 1870, which prohibited individuals from banding together to deprive others of constitutional rights, including freedom of assembly and the right to keep and bear arms. The Court ruled that the Fourteenth Amendment did not empower Congress to protect such rights, and therefore they remain "subject to State jurisdiction"—in other words, rendering those precious rights unprotected. The Southern states and white marauders were unleashed to violate the rights of black citizens with impunity, demonstrating the disastrous human catastrophe that can occur when courts abandon their core role in protecting individual rights and policing the constitutional limits of government.

The apotheosis of judicial abdication came two decades later in *Plessy v. Ferguson*[10] in 1896. By that time, Jim Crow "separate but equal" laws had become ubiquitous throughout the South. A streetcar company bankrolled a test case to challenge the laws requiring separate cars for blacks and whites. The plaintiff, Adolph Plessy, was light skinned and only one-eighth black, but that was enough to consign him to the colored car under the Louisiana law.

The most obvious legal argument—freedom of contract—had been removed from the challengers' arsenal by *Slaughter-House*. That left the more difficult argument that the separate but equal laws violated the equal protection guarantee: more difficult not on conceptual grounds, for the guarantee as written clearly would prevent such unequal laws, but on historical grounds, for legal segregation was widespread and accepted when the Fourteenth Amendment was passed.

Writing for an eight-to-one majority, Justice Henry B. Brown acknowledged that the object of the equal protection clause "was undoubtedly to enforce the absolute equality of the two races before the law," which indeed it was. But in a remarkable and tragic display of judicial obfuscation, he went on to conclude that "in the nature of things, it could not have been intended to abolish distinctions based on color, or to enforce social, as distinguished from political equality, or a commingling of the two races upon terms unsatisfactory to either." Such laws, the Court ruled, are "within the competency of the state legislatures in the exercise of their police power."

Fortunately, there was a dissenting opinion, albeit by a single justice, which laid the groundwork for the logic of *Plessy* to be overturned more than a half century later. Justice John M. Harlan (whose son also would serve on the Court) found that the challenged law was "inconsistent with the personal liberty of citizens, white and black." Harlan affirmed the underlying principles of the equal protection guarantee. "There is no caste here," he proclaimed. "Our Constitution is color-blind, and neither knows nor tolerates classes among citizens. In respect of civil rights, all citizens are equal before the law."

It appeared from *Plessy* that the equal protection clause would go the way of the privileges or immunities clause—to jurisprudential oblivion. Fortunately, that ultimately proved not to be the case. But until *Brown* in 1954, the Court's failure to enforce the equal protection guarantee resulted in the subordination of blacks, women, and others who were not politically powerful.

But that period of jurisprudence was not all dismal. At the same time as the Court was attempting to bury the equal protection clause, Justice Stephen Field, one of the *Slaughter-House* dissenters, was working to protect economic liberty under the due process protection of the Fourteenth Amendment. Those efforts started coming to fruition starting in the final part of the nineteenth century. In 1886, the Court struck down in *Yick Wo v. Hopkins*[11] a San Francisco ordinance that limited laundries to those constructed of bricks or stone, a thinly disguised attempt to drive Chinese entrepreneurs—whose laundries were constructed of wood—out of business. The Court found that the law vested too much discretion in the board of supervisors, holding that "the very idea that one man may be compelled to hold his life, or the means of living, or any material right essential to the enjoyment of life, at the mere will of another, seems to be intolerable in any country where freedom prevails, as being the essence of slavery itself."

Applying the due process guarantee, the Court began to aggressively scrutinize state and local restrictions on freedom of enterprise to determine whether they were legitimate protections of health and safety or instead were excessive, arbitrary, or protectionist. In *Lochner v. New York*[12] in 1905, the Court invalidated a statute that limited employment in bakeries to 10 hours per day and 60 hours per week. Bakery owner Joseph Lochner was convicted under the law. The Court emphasized that the Fourteenth Amendment was not intended to interfere with valid exercises of the states' police power. But it observed that "many laws of this character," enacted ostensibly to protect public health and safety, "are, in reality, passed from other motives." Absent judicial scrutiny, the Court reasoned, "[n]o trade, no occupation, no mode of earning one's living, could escape this all-pervading power . . . although such [regulations] might seriously cripple the ability of the laborer to support himself and his family." The Court concluded that the law was "an unreasonable, unnecessary, and arbitrary interference with the right of the individual to his personal liberty or to enter into those contracts in relation to labor which may seem to him appropriate or necessary for the support of himself and his family."

Justice Oliver Wendell Holmes, one of the most statist justices ever to serve on the Supreme Court, issued a dissenting opinion that, unfortunately, previewed the state of the law with regard to economic liberty that would become ascendant 30 years later and still prevails today. "This case is decided upon an economic theory which a large part of the country does not entertain,"

Holmes declared, namely the "shibboleth" of the "liberty of the citizen to do as he likes so long as he does not interfere with the liberty of others to do the same." A constitution, Holmes asserted, "is not intended to embody a particular economic theory, whether of paternalism and the organic relation of the citizen to the State or of laissez faire. It is made for people of fundamentally differing views."

Indeed, the Constitution does not embrace an express economic theory, although its protection of private property rights and free commerce among the states makes it alien to socialist schemes. But it does explicitly embrace a theory of limited government and individual rights that, if left unprotected by the courts, leads to unchecked majoritarianism and the violation of those rights.

The Court also applied its view of "substantive" due process—that is, that the due process clause protects the substantive rights of life, liberty, and property—outside the realm of economic regulation. In 1925, the Court struck down an Oregon law that required enrollment of all students in public schools. The law was backed by the Ku Klux Klan in order to destroy Catholic schools. The Court concluded in *Pierce v. Society of Sisters*[13] that one of the unenumerated rights protected by the Constitution is "the liberty of parents and guardians to direct the upbringing and education" of their children. "The fundamental theory of liberty upon which all governments in this Union repose," the Court declared, "excludes any general power of the state to standardize its children by forcing them to accept instruction from public teachers only." Although the Court's protection of economic liberty under the due process clause subsequently would be repudiated, *Pierce* and other cases around that time recognizing parental autonomy remain good law today.

Fortunately, despite objections from the likes of Oliver Wendell Holmes, the Supreme Court continued to vigorously enforce constitutional rights and limits, valiantly striking down many of the excesses of the early New Deal, which dramatically sought to expand the powers of the national government and restrict individual liberty. But the Court majority's days were numbered by age and physical infirmities, and its will ultimately was subverted by political pressure in the form of President Franklin Roosevelt's Court-packing scheme.

One of the worst decisions of that period was *Home Building & Loan Association v. Blaisdell*[14] in 1934. Article I, section 10 provides one of the few express limits on state power in the original Constitution, providing that "[n]o State shall . . . pass any . . . Law impairing the Obligation of Contract." Obviously, enforceable contracts are a foundation of both a free society and the rule of law, and this unequivocal prohibition against abrogating contracts makes clear that the framers attached great importance to it.

In *Blaisdell*, the Court reviewed a statute that prevented mortgage companies from foreclosing on defaulted loans for a certain period of time. The law plainly violated the contract clause. The contracts were unquestionably valid. Would the Court enforce them?

By a five-to-four vote, the Court upheld the law. Finding that the constitutional "prohibition is not absolute and is not to be read with literal exactness like a mathematical formula," the majority, in a decision written by Chief Justice Charles Evans

Hughes, ruled that it was permissible for the state to enforce a statute "in directly preventing the immediate and literal enforcement of contractual obligations by a temporary and conditional restraint, where vital public interests would otherwise suffer."

In dissent, Justice George Sutherland rejected both the notion of an "evolving" Constitution and emergency exceptions. "A provision of the Constitution . . . does not mean one thing at one time and an entirely different thing at another time," he proclaimed. By diluting the plain meaning of the clause, Sutherland warned, the decision would give rise to "future gradual and ever-advancing encroachments upon the sanctity of private and public contracts." He was right: subsequent decisions have given the government nearly carte blanche authority to regulate contractual relationships between private parties, rendering the contract clause nearly as much a jurisprudential dead letter as the privileges or immunities clause—and much to the same effect in terms of its adverse ramifications for economic liberty. And soon Sutherland and his fellow dissenters would be gone from the Court, replaced with justices much more sympathetic to the explosive growth of government power.

In *U.S. v. Carolene Products*[15] in 1938, the Court considered the constitutionality of the Filled Milk Act of 1923, which prohibited the shipment in interstate commerce of any milk product that was blended with any fat or oil other than milk fat. The law was overtly protectionist and was used to prevent a company from selling a product called Milnut, which combined condensed milk and coconut oil.

The Court upheld the law, announcing that it would defer to the wisdom of legislators, applying the so-called "rational basis test," under which nearly all challenged economic regulations prevail. But the Court did not stop there. In the decision's infamous footnote 4, the Court stated that while it would strongly presume the constitutionality of economic regulation, it might not extend such deference "when legislation appears on its face to be within a specific prohibition of the Constitution" or where it exhibits "prejudice against discrete and insular minorities."

This remarkable doctrine had two consequences. First, it established different tiers of constitutional rights, each of which would receive different levels of judicial protection, depending (apparently) on the whim of the Court. Despite the Ninth Amendment's protection of "unenumerated" rights—and the Fourteenth Amendment's guarantee of the "privileges or immunities" of citizens—the Court henceforth would apply heightened scrutiny to constitutional protections that are "specific." Even then, it might (as it ultimately did) pick and choose among rights that are expressly protected in the Bill of Rights, relegating the right to keep and bear arms, for instance, to lesser constitutional protection. Second, it consigned economic liberties—such as freedom of contract, freedom of enterprise, and commercial speech—to judicial purgatory. Even though economic liberties are among the most important rights in a free society, they have received little judicial protection in the three-quarters of a century since the New Deal.

At the same time that the Court was eviscerating protections of certain individual rights, it was loosening congressional power from its constitutional tethers. The power of Congress to regulate interstate commerce—bestowed by the framers in order to protect a free national economy—was transformed into an open-ended grant of congressional authority. The Court's metamorphosis from an independent guardian of individual rights and limits on government power into an enabler of the excesses of the executive and legislative branches occurred swiftly and suddenly— and illustrates the type of dramatic shift that could occur with the switch of a single vote on the Supreme Court today.

In 1935, the Court in *Schechter Poultry Corp. v. United States*[16] unanimously invalidated portions of the National Recovery Act, which gave to the executive branch sweeping authority to create "codes of fair competition" in various trades and industries. The law regulated not only interstate commerce but actions that occurred after the commerce was completed, such as the slaughtering of poultry. Speaking for the Court, Chief Justice Charles Evan Hughes acknowledged that "[e]xtraordinary conditions may call for extraordinary remedies" but declared that "[e]xtraordinary conditions do not create or enlarge government power." If the commerce clause was "construed to reach all enterprises and transactions which could be said to have an indirect effect on interstate commerce," the Court warned, "the federal authority would embrace practically all of the activities of the people and the authority of the State over its domestic concerns would exist only by sufferance of the federal government." That warning, of course, would prove prophetic.

Only seven years later, the Court overturned *Schechter* in *Wickard v. Filburn,*[17] upholding the imposition of penalties against a farmer for growing wheat primarily for use by his family and farm animals. The Court expanded congressional authority to any activity that "affects" interstate commerce. Its reasoning was tortured. Even if the wheat was never marketed in interstate commerce, "it supplies a need of the man who grew it which would otherwise be reflected by purchases in the open market." Therefore, the Court concluded, there was "no doubt that Congress may properly have considered that wheat consumed on the farm where grown, if wholly outside the scheme of regulation, would have a substantial effect in defeating and obstructing its purpose to stimulate trade therein at increased prices." Hence, congressional authority under its power to regulate interstate commerce could be applied to a person because of his decision *not* to engage in interstate commerce. Such a pronouncement essentially transformed the Constitution from a grant of limited and express congressional power into a grant of plenary power.

Although the New Deal Court obliterated limits on government power in the realm of economic regulation, fortunately it generally took its responsibilities seriously with regard to civil liberties, especially freedom of speech. In its 1943 decision in *West Virginia State Board of Education v. Barnette*,[18] the Court invalidated on First Amendment grounds the state's policy of requiring a stiff-armed salute to the American flag, which was applied to expel students who were Jehovah's Witnesses. The Court overturned a prior ruling that held that people who were aggrieved by such policies must resort to democratic processes to change them. "If there is any fixed star in our constitutional constellation," declared Justice Robert Jackson for the Court, "it is that no official, high or petty, can prescribe what shall be orthodox in politics, nationalism, religion, or other matters of opinion." He explained, "The very purpose of the Bill of Rights was to withdraw certain subjects from the vicissitudes of political controversy, to place them beyond the reach of majorities and officials and to establish them as legal principles to be applied by the courts. One's right to life, liberty, and property, to free speech, a free press, freedom of worship and assembly, and other fundamental rights may not be submitted to vote; they depend on the outcome of no elections."

But even in the realm of civil liberties, the New Deal Court issued one of the worst decisions ever handed down. In *Korematsu v. United States*,[19] the Court by a six-to-three vote upheld the internment of Japanese citizens, holding that although such action ordinarily "is inconsistent with our basic governmental institutions," the power to protect the nation "must be commensurate with the threatened danger." In dissent, Justice Jackson sounded the essential principle that emergency does not enlarge government's constitutional powers. Even worse than the internment order, Jackson declared, was the Court's decision sustaining it, for "once a judicial decision . . . rationalizes the Constitution to show that [it] sanctions such an order, the Court has for all time validated the principle of racial discrimination." That principle, he continued, "then lies about like a loaded weapon ready for the hand of any authority that can bring forward a plausible claim of urgent need." Of course, that weapon has been discharged time and again since the Court sanctioned such a grievous exception to the equal protection guarantee in *Korematsu*.

With a large number of Supreme Court appointments made during five successive Democratic administrations—and with President Dwight Eisenhower making a major misstep in appointing two of the most liberal justices in the Court's history,

Earl Warren and William Brennan Jr.—the New Deal Court evolved into the equally liberal Warren Court.

To its credit, the Warren Court continued its predecessor's tradition of striking down laws abridging civil liberties—most importantly, *Brown v. Board of Education*,[20] which vindicated the equal protection guarantee in pronouncing that segregated schools were unconstitutional. Similarly, in *Stanley v. Georgia*[21] in 1969, the Court struck down a law criminalizing the private possession of obscene materials in the home. "If the First Amendment means anything, it means that a State has no business telling a man, sitting alone in his own house, what books he may read or what films he may watch," declared Justice Thurgood Marshall, adding, "Our whole constitutional heritage rebels at the thought of giving government the power to control men's minds." In *Wisconsin v. Yoder* three years later,[22] the Court invalidated a compulsory school attendance law as applied to Amish children, holding that the law "affirmatively compels them, under threat of criminal sanction, to perform acts undeniably at odds with fundamental tenets of their religious beliefs." And in the *Virginia Pharmacy* case,[23] the Court struck a blow for commercial speech, invalidating a state law passed at the behest of pharmacists that forbade advertising prescription drug prices. The Court held that the First Amendment compels that courts "assume that this information is not in itself harmful, and that the best means [to protect consumers] is to open the channels of communication rather than to close them."

But the Warren Court also continued the dichotomy between so-called fundamental and nonfundamental rights, protecting the former while allowing governments broad latitude to violate the latter. Even worse, the Court plunged into judicial lawlessness by expanding its powers beyond the judicial realm into the legislative and executive arenas. And it did so with gusto, literally creating rather than interpreting law in multiple important areas of American society.

In *Miranda v. Arizona*,[24] the Court not only struck down coerced interrogations of criminal suspects, but it also created the language that police officers should use to inform suspects of their rights—a classic legislative or executive function that exceeds legitimate judicial power. Likewise, in *Goldberg v. Kelly*,[25] the Court recognized a right to welfare, which since that decision has received far greater judicial protection than the right to earn a living. In the *Swann* decision,[26] the Court approved judicially imposed forced busing of students for desegregation. And, of course, in *Roe v. Wade*,[27] the Court not only struck down state laws prohibiting abortions but also established a trimester system to determine the respective boundaries of women's rights and state powers.

One can agree with the outcomes of some of those landmark Warren Court decisions yet still find oneself profoundly troubled by the "remedies" that were imposed. For they validated the darkest fears of the framers, expressed by Alexander Hamilton in *The Federalist No. 78*, that the judicial branch would become dangerous if it exercised legislative or executive powers. When a court is confronted with an unconstitutional law or government action, its proper response is to strike it down. If government officials continue their unlawful actions, the courts may issue an injunction preventing such actions. But they should never take on legislative or executive functions, for unlike the executive and legislative branches, no constitutional check on their power exists if they do so. For instance, after the Supreme Court struck down school segregation in the 1950s, the courts did not call out the troops to enforce the decision—President Eisenhower did. By contrast, the courts themselves in the 1960s and '70s imposed forced busing and racial quotas, took over school and prison systems, and even imposed taxes.

Such judicial lawlessness eroded the rule of law and the public's support for the judicial system. Political backlash predictably ensued. But rather than impeaching judges, abolishing courts, or forcing judges to explain themselves in congressional hearings, the American people acted to correct judicial lawlessness through the principal mechanism established by the Constitution to do so: by electing presidents who were committed to appointing different judges.

The makeover took some time. President Nixon's appointments of two moderate conservatives, Chief Justice Warren Burger and Justice Lewis Powell, helped curb some of the Warren Court's excesses. His appointment of Justice Harry Blackmun (and President Gerald Ford's appointment of Justice John Paul Stevens) actually fortified the liberal wing of the Court. But it was Nixon's appointment of Justice William Rehnquist that signaled the beginning of a true intellectual shift to the right. President Reagan continued the trend through his appointments of Justices Sandra Day O'Connor, Anthony Kennedy, and Antonin Scalia; and by the time Justice Thomas was confirmed in 1991, the transformation was fairly well complete.

As a result of increased focus on the importance of judicial nominations and a series of outstanding conservative appointments, the dangerous direction established by the New Deal and Warren Courts over a period of more than 50 years was reversed. Over the last two decades, the Supreme Court by and large has lived up to its intended role as a bulwark for the rights of the American people. The direction of the current Court, as the next chapter illustrates, is one that freedom advocates should want very much to preserve and perpetuate by electing presidents committed to the American Constitution and the rule of law.

4

The Supreme Court Today

PRECARIOUS MAJORITY

I N AN AMERICA bitterly and closely divided between red and blue, there are few issues on which conservatives and liberals agree. But there is one major proposition on which right and left converge: that the federal courts are out of control and wrecking America.

Of course, they disagree vehemently in their bills of particulars, but both sides have plenty to complain about. Though they disagree about the symptoms, the diagnosis is the same: rampant judicial activism. The titles of two books written in the past decade, one by a conservative radio show host and the other by a leading liberal legal academic, reflect the common complaint: Mark Levin's *Men in Black: How the Supreme Court is Destroying America*[1] and Cass Sunstein's *Radicals in Robes: Why Extreme Right-Wing Courts are Wrong for America*.[2] For Levin, of course, the Court is too liberal; for Sunstein, it is too conservative; and for both, it is too activist. I believe, by contrast, that the Court is not nearly activist enough in terms of striking down unconstitutional laws. Regardless, far from "destroying" or being "wrong" for America, the U.S. Supreme Court is quite often valiant in protecting our freedoms.

The criticism from the right is more than a bit odd and ironic given that the current U.S. Supreme Court is one of the most significant ongoing legacies of the Reagan and Bush administrations. From the perspective of safeguarding individual liberties and constraining government power, the Court is the best in nearly any of our lifetimes. Yet its majority hangs by the precious thread of a single vote. If the balance shifts, it will tilt the Court in an extreme leftward direction, dramatically altering our nation's course.

While the conservative justices have placed the Court on a positive course, it has not engaged in a full-scale judicial counter-revolution, as some liberals have claimed. The liberal charge that the conservative Court has been activist in the important sense of striking down unconstitutional laws is accurate. Two liberal scholars found that in the final 10 years of the Rehnquist Court (1994–2005), conservative justices were far more likely to vote to strike down congressional laws than were the liberal justices. Leading the way was Justice Clarence Thomas, who voted to invalidate the laws in nearly two-thirds of the cases, followed by Justice Anthony Kennedy who voted to strike them down 64 percent of the time. By contrast, the two nominees of President Bill Clinton, Justices Ruth Bader Ginsburg and Stephen Breyer, voted to strike down the challenged federal laws in 39 and 28 percent of the cases, respectively.[3]

But putting matters into perspective paints a different picture. The Court struck down only a few dozen federal laws during that 10-year period. That may sound like a lot, especially when compared to liberal Courts that were far more deferential to federal power. But it is a drop in the bucket when compared to the explosive growth in the number of federal laws and regulations in recent years. From the ratification of the Constitution in 1789, it took 169 years—until 1958, two decades after the New Deal was codified into law—for the compilation of federal laws in the U.S. Code to reach 11,472 pages. It took only 42 more years, to 2000, to increase that number fourfold. And that does not take into account the mammoth legislation that has been passed during the Obama administration. The growth of federal regulations is even greater: in 1960, all federal regulations were compiled in 22,102 pages; today, they total more than 146,000 pages.[4] Assuming that the legislative and executive branches are creating the same percentage of unconstitutional laws and regulations as they were in the 1950s and '60s, the Supreme Court would have to strike down far more of them just to stay even with past Courts.

In reality, the changes wrought by the Rehnquist and Roberts Courts have been evolutionary, not revolutionary. The Court has overturned very few prior precedents in the past two decades. Among the justices, only Clarence Thomas regularly reexamines past precedents to determine whether they are faithful to constitutional text and intent, which frankly all Supreme Court justices should do.[5]

Nor are all of the significant rulings decided along rigid conservative/liberal lines. For instance, in *Troxel v. Granville*,[6] the Court struck down a Washington law that allowed any person to petition for visitation rights with a child, even over the parent's objection. The Court's majority, an odd-couple alliance consisting of Chief Justice Rehnquist and Justices O'Connor, Souter, Thomas, Ginsburg, and Breyer, applied the rule of *Pierce v. Society of Sisters* that parents have the right to control the upbringing of their children. The dissenters—Justices Stevens, Scalia, and Kennedy— scoffed at the idea of such unenumerated rights. Similarly, a case I argued before the Supreme Court that struck down discriminatory state barriers to direct interstate shipment of wine to consumers produced one of the most unusual lineups in recent years: in the majority were Justices Kennedy, Scalia, Souter, Ginsburg, and Breyer; while Chief Justice Rehnquist and Justices Thomas, Stevens, and O'Connor dissented.[7]

But the five conservatives and four liberals usually vote with each other on contentious cases. Indeed, since Justice Sandra Day O'Connor's retirement, the "swing justice" is Anthony Kennedy, who generally is more conservative than O'Connor was.

Despite its evolutionary approach and a sometimes less-than-cohesive majority, the conservative Court has made profoundly positive changes in constitutional jurisprudence. I will describe briefly seven areas in which the Rehnquist and Roberts Courts have moved jurisprudence closer to the intent of the Constitution: private property rights, racial preferences, school choice, Second Amendment rights, political speech, congressional authority under the commerce clause, and federalism. There are other areas, such as criminal law, where the Rehnquist and Roberts Courts have moved jurisprudence in a rightward direction, but these seven categories are good examples of issues on which the divide between liberal and conservative justices is sharpest, and in which dramatic and negative change can be expected if the liberal justices gain a majority on the Supreme Court.

1. *Private property rights.* Despite multiple express protections of private property rights in the Constitution, liberal courts relegated those vital rights to second-tier status. Governments have been allowed to regulate and even take property largely unfettered by constitutional constraints.

This began to change in 1987 when the Supreme Court ruled in the *Nollan* case[8] that the state could not condition a permit to build an oceanfront house on a requirement that the owners cede public access to the beach. The Court established the proposition that if a community desires a public good, it may not impose the entire cost of securing that good upon discrete property owners, unless there is an "essential nexus" between the permit sought and the public good. The state "may well be right that [public access] is a good idea," remarked Justice Scalia, "but that does not establish that the Nollans . . . alone can be compelled to contribute to its realization."

Five years later, the Court held that South Carolina's regulation preventing a property owner from constructing any significant structure on his beachfront property, which essentially reduced the property value to zero, amounted to a taking requiring compensation under the Fifth Amendment.[9] After being forced to bear the cost of acquiring the property rather than imposing the costs of the desired public good on the property owner, the state decided that the rational thing to do with the property was to sell it for development.

And in *Dolan v. City of Tigard*,[10] the Court ruled against a city's efforts to require the owner of a hardware store, as a condition of receiving a permit to expand, to build a bicycle path and dedicate property to a greenway. In a decision by Chief Justice Rehnquist, the Court demanded "rough proportionality" between the exaction demanded in exchange for the permit and the "nature and extent [of] the proposed development."

Together, these and other decisions recognized that government regulation can represent a de facto "taking" of private property, and they helped constrain the widespread extortionist practices of state and local governments.

But the Court failed to fully revitalize the Fifth Amendment's takings clause. In the infamous *Kelo v. City of New London* decision,[11] Justice Kennedy inexplicably joined the four liberal justices[12] to uphold a redevelopment agency's decision to bulldoze a working-class neighborhood to make way for amenities for a Pfizer plant.[13] Over the years, the Fifth Amendment's requirement that private property may only be taken for "public use" had been whittled down to a much more permissive showing of a "public benefit." The majority opinion in *Kelo* by Justice Stevens acknowledged that, in early American jurisprudence, public use meant public use; but he observed that "that narrow view steadily eroded over time," because "it proved to be impractical given the diverse and always evolving needs of society." In dissent, Justice Thomas declared that "I do not believe this Court can eliminate liberties expressly enumerated in the Constitution," lamenting that the decision "is simply the latest in a string of our cases construing the Public Use Clause to be a virtual nullity, without the slightest nod to its original meaning."

Perhaps more than any other case, *Kelo* illustrates the gaping chasm between the conservative and liberal justices on the Court, the huge difference that a single vote can make, and the tragic human consequences that can flow from an abdication of the Court's most important function. In essence, the Court crafted a judicial amendment to the Constitution, through which the plain meaning of an important constraint on government power was erased, giving local governments broad discretion to engage in grassroots tyranny. Despite *Kelo*, the conservative Court has placed property rights on firmer jurisprudential ground. Should the Court's balance change from conservative to liberal, we can expect a wholesale evisceration of the property rights protections that are central to our free society.

2. *Racial preferences*. The ghosts of two of the most reviled Supreme Court decisions—*Plessy* and *Korematsu*—still lurk around the edges of American jurisprudence, sanctioning the notion that, despite the Fourteenth Amendment's guarantee of equal protection under law, it is sometimes justifiable to classify individuals and assign benefits and burdens on the basis of race or ethnicity.

For many years the Court has recognized that classifications that touch upon race or ethnicity, just like those that infringe fundamental rights, are subject to "strict scrutiny"—that is, they are permissible only if they are narrowly tailored to advance a compelling government purpose. Few government actions survive strict scrutiny.

Fortunately, the Rehnquist and Roberts Courts have made significant progress in eradicating the color line from American law. But the situation they inherited was muddled at best. As the issue of "affirmative action" began reaching the Court in the 1970s, it refused to clearly apply strict scrutiny because the discrimination it inflicted was "benign." In the 1978 *Bakke* decision,[14] liberal and conservative justices split four to four over whether to uphold an explicit racial quota system for admissions to a state medical school. The deciding justice, Lewis Powell, concluded that strict racial quotas were unconstitutional but that the school could take race into account as one factor in the admissions process. The decision opened a Pandora's box, allowing admissions officials to apply racial preferences so long as they did not do so openly.

In 1986, the Court by a five-to-four vote applied strict scrutiny in the context of racial preferences for the first time, striking down race-conscious teacher layoffs.[15] Three years later, the Court invalidated a 30 percent minority set-aside for public contracts in *City of Richmond v. J.A. Croson Co.*[16] Later, in *Adarand Constructors, Inc. v. Pena*,[17] the Court overturned a past decision upholding federal contract set-asides, which had applied an intermediate standard of review. In a concurring opinion, Justice Scalia declared, "To pursue the concept of racial entitlement— even for the most admirable and benign of purposes—is to reinforce and preserve for future mischief the way of thinking that produced race slavery, race privilege and race hatred." Echoing Justice Harlan's dissent in *Plessy* nearly a century before, Scalia concluded, "In the eyes of government, we are just one race here. It is American."

But though the Court clearly embraced the notion that all racial classifications are subject to strict judicial scrutiny, it refused to abolish them altogether. In *Gratz v. Bollinger*,[18] the Court invalidated a University of Michigan undergraduate admissions scheme that automatically awarded to certain minority candidates 20 of the 100 points necessary for admission. But Justice O'Connor switched sides in a companion case, *Grutter v. Bollinger*,[19] joining with a five-to-four majority to uphold a law school admissions system in which race was used as a factor in individual cases to create a "critical mass" of minority students. Justice Kennedy in his dissenting opinion ridiculed the Court's rationale, saying that the amorphous concept of a "critical mass" is "a delusion used by the Law School to mask its attempt to make race an automatic factor in most instances and to achieve numerical goals indistinguishable from quotas."

O'Connor attempted to reassure skeptics by saying that "[w]e expect that 25 years from now, the use of racial preferences will no longer be necessary to further the interest approved today." But the effect of the Court's decision, observed Justice Thomas in dissent, was to "grant a 25-year license to violate the Constitution. . . . For the immediate future, however, the majority has placed its imprimatur on a practice that can only weaken the principle of equality embodied in our Declaration of Independence and the Equal Protection Clause."

Justice O'Connor's retirement and replacement by a more conservative justice may accelerate the 25-year time frame, bringing America finally to the point where racial classifications of all types are forbidden. However, a different fate awaits if liberals gain a majority on the Supreme Court. Although Justice Stephen Breyer voted with the majority striking down an overt quota in *Gratz*, the liberals have made clear that they would approve all types of covert race-conscious government decision making. The tremendous progress America has painstakingly made in race relations could be reversed by a liberal Supreme Court majority, replacing the promise of equal opportunity with a divisive racial spoils system.

3. *School choice.* Over the last several decades, as public schools increasingly have failed to provide adequate education to millions

of American schoolchildren, education reformers have attempted to expand school choices. Their efforts have been fiercely resisted by powerful special-interest groups that benefit from the status quo and are determined to preserve the status quo regardless of its human consequences. One of their weapons is legal challenges, particularly against school choice programs that allow children to enroll in private schools. Between 1990, when the first urban school choice program was created, until 2002, when the U.S. Supreme Court finally lifted the federal constitutional cloud from school choice, teachers' unions and their allies challenged an array of school choice programs across the country, focusing on the First Amendment.[20]

The First Amendment contains two prohibitions against government action concerning religion: it may not abridge the "free exercise" of religion nor "establish" religion. The plain meaning of these two provisions, along with the historical context of state-established religion, yields two principles. First, that the government should pursue a neutral course toward religion, neither interfering with its free exercise nor establishing it. Second, that it should not favor a particular church or religion over nonreligion.

What neither constitutional language nor history suggest is what the First Amendment was transformed into during the Warren era: a "wall of separation" between the government and religion. If there is one area of constitutional law that is conceptually confused beyond any other, it is the jurisprudence surrounding the establishment clause. Precedents are hopelessly subjective, often focusing on whether there is a "symbolic" union between church and state.

At a time when virtually all education was private and often religiously based, it is odd to imagine that the framers would have been offended by efforts to place aid at the disposal of families to decide where best to educate their children. But when school choice activists began their efforts in earnest, they were saddled with a Warren Court precedent, the 1973 *Nyquist* decision,[21] which struck down state aid programs for private schools because the Court concluded that their "primary effect" was to advance religion.

Ten years later, with an emerging conservative majority, the Court upheld tuition tax deductions in Minnesota, despite the fact that the vast majority were used in religious schools.[22] "The historic purposes of the [Establishment] Clause," Justice Rehnquist explained in his majority opinion, "simply do not encompass the sort of attenuated financial benefit, ultimately controlled by the private choices of individual parents, that eventually flows to parochial schools from the neutrally available tax benefit at issue in this case."

Over a series of cases, the Court continued to refine establishment clause jurisprudence, focusing on the principles of government neutrality toward religion, voluntary individual choices, and an absence of coercion. When a school voucher case finally reached the Court in 2002, all eyes were on Justice O'Connor, who was the often-unpredictable swing justice in establishment clause cases. But she showed no hesitation in signing on to the landmark *Zelman v. Simmons-Harris*[23] decision upholding vouchers for low-income students in Cleveland. Where "a government aid program is neutral with respect to religion, and provides assistance to a broad class of citizens who, in turn, direct government aid to religious schools wholly as a result of their own genuine and independent private choice," declared Chief Justice Rehnquist in the majority opinion, "it is not readily subject to challenge under the Establishment Clause."

Far more remarkable than the majority opinion, which was consistent with a long line of recent precedents as well as with constitutional language and precedent, were the dissenting opinions of the four liberal justices, which were downright histrionic. Justice Stevens raised the specter of "religious strife" of the type seen in "the Balkans, Northern Ireland, and the Middle East"—concerns echoed by Justice Breyer's warnings of "religiously based social conflict." Far from the rioting in the streets predicted by the liberal dissenters, the only thing that has happened in Cleveland is that low-income children are enjoying better education. Breyer's dissent was especially troublesome given his professed devotion to judicial restraint and to "active liberty"—the process through which communities express their values and to which, Breyer asserts, the judiciary ought to show deference, except apparently when the community chooses to adopt public policy such as school vouchers that is at odds with Breyer's preferences. What the vehemence of the dissents demonstrates is the tremendous likelihood that with an additional liberal justice, the Supreme Court would strike down school choice programs, thereby dooming the hopes and aspirations of generations of economically disadvantaged children.

4. *Second Amendment rights.* Although the liberal courts from the 1930s through the 1980s purported to view rights as fundamental if they were expressly guaranteed by the Bill of Rights,

they made an exception for the Second Amendment's right to keep and bear arms.

The Roberts Court removed this anomaly. In 2008, the Court ruled by a five-to-four vote in *District of Columbia v. Heller*[24] that the Second Amendment protects the right of individuals to possess firearms for purposes such as self-defense within the home. Although certain regulations of gun ownership might be valid, the Court held that the District's complete ban on handguns violated that right.

All four liberal justices dissented. Justice Breyer wrote that even if the Second Amendment protects individuals' rights, these rights should be balanced against the government's interests in regulating or prohibiting firearms. The majority opinion by Justice Scalia rejected that approach. "We know of no other enumerated constitutional right whose core protection has been subjected to a freestanding 'interest-balancing' approach," Scalia observed. Thus did the Court eliminate the dichotomy among liberties guaranteed by the Bill of Rights.

But one more important issue remained. Most of the Bill of Rights by its terms restricts the federal government, not states. Previous Court decisions had held that other protections of the Bill of Rights were "incorporated" through the Fourteenth Amendment's due process clause to the states. But the incorporation was selective and had not yet encompassed the Second Amendment. *Heller* was limited to the District of Columbia. It took another case to apply the Second Amendment to the states.

Two years later, in *McDonald v. Chicago*,[25] the Court took that additional step, invalidating Chicago's handgun ban. The plaintiffs argued that the Bill of Rights should have been incorporated to the states not through the Fourteenth Amendment's due process clause but through its privileges or immunities clause—a position that Justice Thomas embraced in a powerful concurring opinion that called into question the continuing validity of the notorious *Slaughter-House Cases*, the 1873 ruling that obliterated the privileges or immunities clause. The other conservative justices found it unnecessary to overturn *Slaughter-House* but subjected it to strong criticism, which could come in handy in a future case seeking to reestablish judicial protection for economic liberty. The Court majority had no difficulty concluding that the individual right to keep and bear arms recognized in *Heller* should apply to the states.

Once again, the liberal justices dissented. Justice Breyer asserted that "the Framers did not write the Second Amendment in order to protect a private right of armed self defense. There has been, and is, no consensus that the right is, or was, 'fundamental.'"

The position of the liberal justices suggests that if they gain a majority, the individual right to keep and bear arms once again will be lost. Even worse, the liberal justices demonstrate a very disturbing propensity to pick and choose among protected rights. Even the line of demarcation suggested in the early days of the New Deal Court—between rights that are expressly protected in the Bill of Rights and those that are not—has fallen by the wayside. Entitlements such as welfare would be protected while explicitly enumerated liberties such as the right to keep and bear arms and private property rights would not. Under such a subjective system, we no longer would have the rule of law but the rule of judges.

5. *Political speech.* Nearly all constitutional scholars on both left and right agree that political speech is at the core of the First Amendment's free-speech guarantee. It is curious, then, that so many on the left are eager to restrict it, subsidize it, monitor and regulate it—everything except to allow the unfettered flow of political expression in the world's most vibrant democracy.

In *The Federalist No. 10*, James Madison observed that there are two ways to control the evils of faction: either suppress factions themselves or prevent them from executing schemes that detract from the common good. The first solution, he argued, is worse than the disease, because it restricts essential political liberties. Rather, he favored constitutional mechanisms to check the ability of special interests to carry out their schemes of oppression.

Sadly, we have not followed Madison's advice. We have allowed government at every level to grow and have done little to control the ability of special interests to manipulate the levers of government for their own ends. Instead, we have suppressed the ability—not just of special-interest groups but of all Americans—to participate fully and freely in the political process.

The Court's failure to fully protect political speech traces to its muddled 1976 decision in *Buckley v. Valeo*,[26] in which it sustained federal limits on individual campaign contributions as well as disclosure and reporting requirements while striking down restrictions on campaign spending, expenditures by independent groups, and self-financing of campaigns. The mixed outcome helped create the perverse situation we have today, in which individual campaign contributions are strictly limited while shadowy independent committees spend vast amounts of money on campaigns.

Campaign-related speech is one area where there is a sharp distinction between the Rehnquist Court, which continued the *Buckley* decision's approach, and the Roberts Court, which has been much more vigilant in enforcing First Amendment guarantees. In 2002, Congress enacted the McCain-Feingold law, which imposed a ban on unrestricted "soft money" contributions to political parties by unions, corporations, or wealthy individuals; limited advertising by unions, corporations, and nonprofit groups up to 60 days before an election; and restricted the ability of political parties to use funds to advertise on behalf of candidates. Although expressing reservations about the bill's constitutionality, President George W. Bush signed it into law, apparently assuming that the Court would correct the flaws.

It did not. In *McConnell v. Federal Election Commission*,[27] the Court, with Justice O'Connor siding with the liberal justices, sustained most of the act.

But once O'Connor retired and was replaced by Justice Alito, the Court moved firmly to bring regulations of campaign-related speech into compliance with the First Amendment. In *Randall v. Sorrell*,[28] the Court struck down Vermont's extremely low individual contribution limits, although it reaffirmed the holding of *Buckley* that such limits are permissible if they do not unduly restrict contributions. Justice Breyer joined the conservative justices in the six-to-three decision.

In 2010, the Court revisited part of the McCain-Feingold law in the landmark *Citizens United*[29] decision. The case arose from a dispute over a movie made by a nonprofit group about then senator Hillary Clinton, which was banned from broadcast within 30 days of the 2008 presidential primaries, in which Clinton was running. The Court overturned part of the *McConnell* decision and invalidated the ban, but the broader impact was its recognition that corporations have a right to engage in political speech. "If the First Amendment has any force," wrote Justice Anthony Kennedy in the five-to-four decision split along philosophical lines, "it prohibits Congress from fining or jailing citizens, or associations of citizens, for simply engaging in political speech."

More recently, the Court invalidated part of Arizona's public campaign finance law in a case litigated by my Goldwater Institute colleague Nick Dranias.[30] In addition to providing a government subsidy for participating candidates, the scheme provided matching funds for candidates whose nonsubsidized opponents spent beyond the base subsidy levels and for independent expenditures made on behalf of nonsubsidized candidates. In essence, when privately funded candidates were raising contributions for their own campaigns, they also were triggering taxpayer funding for their opponents. The five-to-four conservative majority found that the matching funds penalized privately funded candidates and placed the government's thumb on the election scales.

The liberal dissent was penned by Justice Elena Kagan, who argued that the specter of corruption was sufficient to warrant this type of government intervention in the political marketplace. "The First Amendment's core purpose," she declared, "is to foster a healthy, vibrant political system full of robust discussion and debate." The government can aid that purpose, she asserted, even by going beyond the role of referee or policeman and becoming an active participant in the electoral process, not only through public financing but also by ensuring that candidates have equal resources.

Justice Kagan's vision sounds more like a socialist system than a democratic one. Were her views to prevail, it is difficult to imagine any constraint on government's ability to level the playing field or even tilt it in favor of candidates and other participants in the political process who are willing to play the game the way the government thinks it should be played.

6. *Congressional authority under the commerce clause.* Perhaps on no other issue are the practical ramifications of the divide between conservative and liberal justices more salient than in the realm of federal power under the commerce clause. This owes to the radical transformation of the Constitution effectuated by the New Deal Court. The framers clearly had intended to confer narrow and express powers upon the national government. Without benefit of a constitutional amendment, the New Deal Court removed any meaningful limitation on those powers by allowing the national government to regulate anything that "affects" interstate commerce, no matter how remotely. As Congress and federal regulatory agencies constantly seek to expand their power—a process reflected by the unprecedented federal healthcare legislation and the thousands of regulations that can be expected to flow from it—determinations of the limits of federal power (or lack thereof) under the commerce clause will be crucially important.

The Rehnquist Court began to slowly retether congressional power to constitutional language and intent. In *United States v. Lopez*[31] in 1995, the Court invalidated the Gun-Free School Zones Act. In a decision by Chief Justice Rehnquist divided on philosophical lines, the Court found that the key question in determining whether congressional authority exists to regulate an activity rests upon whether it "'substantially affects' interstate commerce." The regulation of guns in school zones, the Court concluded, "by its terms has nothing to do with 'commerce' or any sort of economic enterprise" and "is not an essential part of a larger regulation of economic activity." Were the challenged law to stand, the Court reasoned, "we are hard pressed to posit any activity by an individual that Congress is without power to regulate."

Five years later, the Court reached a similar result in striking down the Violence Against Women Act as exceeding congressional power under the commerce clause in *United States v. Morrison*.[32] The law allowed rape victims to sue their assailants in federal court, notwithstanding the existence of legal actions in state courts. The Court held that Congress could not "regulate noneconomic, violent criminal conduct based solely on that conduct's aggregate effect on interstate commerce."

But the Court reversed course in 2005 in *Gonzales v. Raich*,[33] in which Justices Kennedy and Scalia joined with their liberal colleagues in a six-to-three decision allowing Congress to criminalize the production and use of homegrown marijuana even where states allow it for medicinal purposes. In so doing, the Court fortified the precedential vitality of one of the worst New Deal cases, *Wickard v. Filburn*. Scalia justified his opinion on the grounds that allowing the states to legalize medicinal marijuana would undercut the federal regulation of interstate commerce.

Chief Justice Rehnquist and Justices O'Connor and Thomas strongly disagreed. "Relying on Congress' abstract assertions, the

Court has endorsed making it a federal crime to grow small amounts of marijuana in one's own home for one's own medicinal use," Justice O'Connor observed. "This overreaching stifles an express choice by some States, concerned for the lives and liberties of their people, to regulate marijuana differently." Justice Thomas, as always, examined the original intent of the commerce power. "Certainly no evidence from the founding suggests that 'commerce' included the mere possession of a good or some personal activity that did not involve trade or exchange for value," he proclaimed. "If the Federal Government can regulate growing a half-dozen cannabis plants for personal consumption (not because it is interstate commerce, but because it is inextricably bound up with interstate commerce), then [congressional powers] have no meaningful limits."

It remains to be seen whether the Roberts Court will continue the course of returning the commerce power to its constitutional moorings or tragically abandoning the quest. But one thing is certain: the liberal justices are absolutely dedicated to the proposition that the federal government's regulatory power is essentially unlimited. Indeed, questions about these issues are so central to liberal ideology that they figured prominently in Chief Justice Roberts's confirmation hearings. If we have any hope of restoring limitations to the power of the federal government to regulate our lives, it exists only so long as a conservative majority remains on the Supreme Court.

7. *Federalism.* To a large degree, federalism is the flip side of congressional authority under the commerce clause: the federal government may not have power in a particular instance either because that power was not delegated to it in the Constitution *or*

because the states retained that authority. The reservation of all powers in the states that were not expressly delegated to the national government was made clear in the Tenth Amendment.

The New Deal and Warren Courts dismissed the Tenth Amendment as a mere "truism," an historical anachronism that had no independent vitality in constraining the power of the national government. Fortunately, the Roberts Court has restored a significant measure of state autonomy. Even more fortuitously, this is an enterprise occasionally supported by liberal justices, who sometimes support the authority of states to dissent from federal orthodoxy in fashioning distinctive public policy.

Federalism issues often arise in the context of whether federal law "preempts" conflicting state law. In previous Courts, the answer nearly always was yes. By contrast, the Roberts Court has gone out of its way to avoid finding such conflicts so as not to invalidate state laws.

In *Gonzales v. Oregon*,[34] the Court upheld Oregon's assisted-suicide law against a federal preemption challenge by the Bush administration. The lineup was atypical, with Justices Stevens, Kennedy, O'Connor, Ginsburg, and Breyer voting to sustain the law; while Chief Justice Roberts and Justices Scalia and Kennedy dissented. The Court noted that within "the structure and limitations of federalism," the regulation of health and safety, including medical standards, traditionally has been a state rather than federal concern. Finding federal preemption, the Court ruled, would mark "a radical shift of authority from the States to the Federal Government to define general standards of medical practice in every locality."

Three years later, in *Horne v. Flores*,[35] the Court divided five to four along conservative/liberal lines against a federal court injunction prohibiting Arizona from pursuing its English-only education policy. The Court held that federal courts should tread lightly in "areas of core state responsibility, such as public education" and that "federalism concerns are heightened when . . . a federal court decree has the effect of dictating state or local budget priorities."

That same year, the Court construed section 5 of the Voting Rights Act to allow a Texas utility district to "bail out" from coverage under the law.[36] Section 5 was supposed to be a temporary provision aimed at recalcitrant states that could be counted on to resist the protections of the Voting Rights Act. Such jurisdictions would be forced to submit all changes that affect voting—even municipal annexations or changes in the location of polling places—to the U.S. Department of Justice for "pre-clearance." Despite the fact that the conditions underlying the emergency provision have receded and that compliance is costly and intrusive, Congress continues to extend the provisions of section 5 to the covered jurisdictions. Rather than strike down section 5, four liberal justices joined four conservatives to broadly construe the language allowing jurisdictions to bail out from the provision's coverage. Justice Thomas went even further in his dissent, declaring that section 5 is altogether unconstitutional.[37]

And in *Chamber of Commerce v. Whiting*,[38] the Court, in a decision authored by Justice Samuel Alito, voted five to three to uphold Arizona's employer sanctions law, despite the fact that Congress possesses express constitutional authority to regulate immigration. The Court found that the state's regulations did not interfere with the federal regulatory scheme and that Arizona had an interest in policing illegal immigration.

One of the most promising cases regarding federalism also was decided in 2011, illustrating that unusual cases often produce important constitutional principles. *Bond v. United States*[39] presented the case of Carol Bond, whose husband had an affair and impregnated his mistress. Mrs. Bond promised to make the other woman's life "a living hell," and she did. Among other things, Bond was videotaped placing poison in the muffler of the other woman's car, for which she was indicted in federal court under the Chemical Weapons Convention of 1993. Because the prosecution arguably interfered with the right of the state to prosecute Bond under its own laws, Bond raised a Tenth Amendment claim, which the lower court dismissed on the grounds that only states have standing to raise Tenth Amendment claims.

The Supreme Court reversed, holding that where an individual's rights are implicated by a federal action, that person can raise the state's sovereign powers as a defense under the Tenth Amendment. This landmark ruling gives individuals a potentially powerful weapon to challenge overzealous federal government actions. Making the case especially noteworthy is the fact that it is one of the few landmark Supreme Court cases resolving important issues of federalism and individual rights to command the votes of all nine justices.

A Painful Prognosis

The unanimity of the *Bond* decision is the rare exception that proves the rule: although the liberal justices sometimes side with structural constitutional limits on government power and with individual rights, too often they do not. For our Constitution and the rule of law it enshrines to endure in our nation's third century, requires the appointment of justices who are firmly committed to underlying constitutional principles.

The sharp divide between liberals and conservatives outlined in the seven categories above carries over into other important areas of law. Some critics assail the conservative majority for failing in some cases, particularly those involving terrorism and the rights of criminal defendants, to sufficiently safeguard individual rights. But however one looks at it, this is not a close question: on the whole, the conservative justices are much more likely than their liberal colleagues to enforce restraints on government power and protect individual rights.

The differences are so profound that a shift of a single justice would mark a dramatically different course. Assuming that Justice Breyer did not leave the Court, he would become the swing justice on a Court with a liberal majority. Although Breyer joins the conservatives more often than the other liberal justices, he is also probably the most likely among all nine justices to sustain the exercise of government power. Although conservatives often are critical of Justice Kennedy, who currently usually casts the swing vote, he is far more conservative than Justice Breyer and even more conservative than Justice O'Connor, who most often held the decisive vote before him. Most important, Kennedy often exhibits libertarian instincts and is among the justices most likely to strike down government power.

The coming presidential elections will probably prove decisive in the Supreme Court's future direction. Two conservative justices and two liberal justices currently are in their 70s. If a Democratic president has the opportunity to replace one or two conservative justices, it will tilt the Court sharply to the left, and it will probably be impossible to change that balance for 20 or 30 years. Likewise, if a Republican president gets to replace one or two liberal justices, it could reinforce the Court's current conservative direction for another generation.

Many Americans believe, with much justification, that there is not much difference between our two major political parties. The number of political independents (myself among them) continues to grow. Even many within the two major parties are not always inspired by their parties' nominees. But however philosophically impure the parties' presidential nominees may be, the appointment of judges presents a very real difference between the parties. No matter who the nominees are, a vote for the Republican candidate is a vote for a conservative judiciary, and a vote for the Democratic nominee is a vote for a liberal judiciary.

This reality renders voting for a third party—or not voting at all—a very serious abstention from a very important decision. In particular, conservatives and libertarians who consider themselves constitutionalists may do grave harm to the Constitution by casting their votes for third-party candidates rather than voting for the major-party candidate who, whatever his or her shortcomings on other issues, will appoint judges who take seriously their oath to uphold the Constitution.

The stakes in the coming presidential elections could not be higher. Our presidents hold their offices fleetingly. Our federal legislators hold their offices at the will and whim of the electorate. Our federal judges, however, hold their positions for life. They are being appointed at a younger age and living longer than ever before. The cases they decide deeply and directly affect the rights and opportunities of every American. The shaping of the judiciary is often the most important decision a president will make. Yet who will hold the power to make judicial nominations is a question that voters rarely take into account in casting their votes in national elections. They should, for there is nothing more consequential or enduring that their votes will decide. It is to raising the visibility of this important decision that this small book is dedicated.

Postscript

. . . AND STATE COURTS, TOO

W HEN AMERICANS THINK of their constitution, they automatically think of the United States Constitution. Few even consider the fact that the vast majority of Americans—all of us who live in one of the 50 states—have not one constitution but two. Few of us learn about our state constitutions in civics classes. The vast majority of law students do not even hear the words "state constitutions" uttered, much less study about them. And for all of their professed devotion to federalism, most conservative public-interest law firms tend to focus their resources almost entirely on federal constitutional issues.

All of which is bizarre considering the central role that state constitutions played in our nation's founding and the role that they continue to play in American law. State constitutions preexisted the federal constitution. The Bill of Rights was based on similar protections in state constitutions. Most of the guarantees of rights and constraints on government power in the U.S. Constitution were not originally extended to the states, because state constitutions were considered the primary bulwarks for the protection of liberty. Together with the U.S. Constitution, state constitutions were thought to provide a "double security" for the rights of the people.

Today, state constitutions provide enormous untapped potential for advancing freedom, for a variety of reasons. The U.S. Supreme Court has recognized that the federal constitution provides a floor for the protection of individual rights. State courts are free to provide greater (though not lesser) protection to rights in their own constitutions that are identical with or similar to federal constitutional guarantees. That potential is especially meaningful with regard to provisions that have been judicially extricated from the federal constitution—such as the privileges or immunities clause, the contracts clause, and the public use requirement of the Fifth Amendment—but often have counterparts in state constitutions. State courts are free to vigorously enforce such provisions in state constitutions even if federal courts refuse to enforce the same provisions in the federal constitution.

Moreover, state constitutions are chock-full of limitations on government power and protections of individual rights that are completely unknown to the federal constitution. For instance, state constitutions often prohibit "private or local bills"—the type of pork-barrel legislation that proliferates at the federal level. Many state constitutions have "gift clauses" that prohibit corporate subsidies. If the U.S. Constitution contained such provisions, earmarks in federal budgets and corporate bailouts would be unconstitutional.

These would be held unconstitutional, that is, if taxpayers had standing to enforce them. But as federal courts have interpreted the Constitution's "case or controversy" requirement for federal jurisdiction, taxpayers do not have standing to challenge unlawful spending or other actions in federal courts. They are forced to resort to the political process to have any recourse. By contrast, in most states, taxpayers have standing to challenge illegal spending and other government actions.

Beyond that, state constitutions generally can be amended more easily than the U.S. Constitution. And although state court precedents are not binding beyond state boundaries, courts in one state often look to the decisions of courts in other states to aid interpretation of similar constitutional provisions. The sum is that state constitutions can provide an independent basis and tremendous opportunity to protect individual rights and restrain the power of government.

Liberals were the first to recognize the enormous potential of state constitutions and to engage in strategic state constitutional litigation. As the federal judiciary started growing more conservative in the 1970s and '80s, Justice William Brennan wrote a pair of seminal law review articles[1] urging liberal activists to take recourse to state constitutions to advance an agenda that was no longer faring so well in the federal courts. He observed that "more state courts are construing state constitutional counterparts of provisions of the Bill of Rights as guaranteeing citizens of their states even more protection than the federal provisions, even those identically phrased," which "is surely an important and highly significant development for our constitutional jurisprudence and for our concept of federalism."

As Brennan observed, "This rebirth in the interest in state constitutional law should be greeted with equal enthusiasm by all those who support our federal system, liberals and conservatives alike." He noted that "those who regard judicial review as inconsistent with our democratic system . . . should find constitutional interpretation by the state judiciary far less objectionable than activist intervention by their federal counterparts." Many state judges, he pointed out, are subject to election, and state constitutions generally are easier to amend than the federal Constitution, hence more democratic mechanisms exist to check the power of state judges than of federal judges.

Liberal advocates heeded Justice Brennan's call to arms with gusto. Criminal defense lawyers, in particular, developed additional protections in state constitutions. But they also successfully expanded other constitutional provisions. For instance, after the U.S. Supreme Court rejected claims for equal education funding under the U.S. Constitution,[2] courts in a number of states, including California, New York, and New Jersey, found that equal school funding was required by state constitutions.

While liberals often have litigated state constitutional provisions, conservatives typically have not. That is especially curious and disappointing given that state constitutions often provide legal tools by which the power of government can be constrained and individual rights (including the rights of taxpayers) can be protected.

My education in state constitutional law came not in law school but at the hands of the teachers' unions. When the first urban school choice program was adopted in Milwaukee in 1990, it was limited to secular private schools. Hence, it was not subject to challenge under the First Amendment. So although we knew a legal challenge was coming, my colleagues and I had no idea what the constitutional basis would be. When the lawsuit was filed, it was based primarily on the "private or local bill" prohibition in the Wisconsin Constitution, on the grounds that the law was adopted as part of the state budget, rather than as a stand-alone bill. Although I spent years defending that program (ultimately successfully), I began to recognize that in many circumstances, the private or local bill clause could provide an important weapon for conservative advocates seeking to challenge pork-barrel or other special-interest legislation.

When school choice programs were adopted that encompassed religious school options, the constitutional challenges expanded as well. Not only did the teachers' unions and their allies invoke the First Amendment, but they also challenged the programs based on the religion provisions of state constitutions, many of which have language that differs from the establishment clause. In particular, the unions relied on the so-called "Blaine amendments," which are found in about three dozen state constitutions. The amendments, mostly adopted in the late nineteenth century, were fueled by anti-Catholic sentiment and aimed at preventing government aid or support of "sectarian" schools (Catholic schools, in the lexicon of the day).

Although we successfully defended school vouchers in the U.S. Supreme Court in 2002, state courts since then in Florida, Arizona, and Colorado have invalidated school choice programs under different provisions of their respective state constitutions—all of which underscores the importance of such provisions.

In 2007, I joined the Goldwater Institute in Arizona to launch the first litigation center within a state-based market-oriented public policy organization.[3] Since then, similar policy groups in Maine, Michigan, North Dakota, Nevada, Ohio, Washington State, Wisconsin, and other states have started litigation centers as well. Given that market-oriented policy groups exist in all 50 states, prospects for further expansion are substantial.

Two Arizona cases that my colleagues and I litigated illustrate especially well the vast potential for litigation by freedom advocates in the state constitutional arena.

At the same time that Suzette Kelo and her neighbors in New London, Connecticut, were fighting eminent domain in the federal courts, a man named Randy Bailey was receiving an eviction notice from the city of Mesa, Arizona, which wanted to take the property occupied by his brake service in order to make way for an expanded hardware store. Although the facts of the two cases were similar—the local governments in both instances were playing Robin Hood in reverse, wielding the power of eminent domain to take property from working-class owners for the benefit of wealthier and more politically powerful interests—the outcomes were starkly different.

That result is attributable to the Arizona Constitution, which provides that "private property shall not be taken for private use."[4] While the U.S. Supreme Court was reading the federal constitution to provide no remedy for Suzette Kelo, the Arizona Court of Appeals was ruling in favor of Randy Bailey under its state constitution. "The federal constitution provides considerably less protection against eminent domain than our Constitution provides," the court declared. "Not every combination of perceived public benefits and advantages will satisfy the 'public use' requirement of our Constitution."[5] As a result of the Arizona court's independent interpretation of its own constitution, while Suzette Kelo's neighborhood is wiped out, Randy Bailey continues to sell brakes at the corner of Country Club and Main Street in Mesa, Arizona.

Whatever the protection (or lack thereof) for private property rights under the U.S. Constitution, states in our federalist system are free to give them greater protection under their state constitutions. In Arizona, as in other states that have independently construed their state constitutions to similar effect, private property rights enjoy far more sanctity than in other states. The potential to secure such protection exists for other important freedoms as well.

At the time we started our litigation center at the Goldwater Institute in 2007, Arizona was rife with corporate subsidies. In particular, local governments were giving copious amounts of taxpayer money to developers to locate retail shopping on their side of municipal borders so as to increase sales-tax revenues. From an economic perspective, the practice was insane, because retail follows rooftops and governments generally do not have to bribe businesses to sell things. But with the self-destructive subsidy wars, taxpayer money was going into the pockets of developers rather than into municipal coffers.

During that time, a Chicago developer came to Phoenix demanding a $100 million subsidy to build a lavish shopping center called CityNorth. The plans were so grandiose that my

Goldwater Institute colleagues and I dubbed the project the "Taj Mah-Mall."

Were this a federally subsidized project, taxpayers would have had no legal recourse. But fortunately, the Arizona Constitution (along with numerous other state constitutions) contains a provision prohibiting gifts of public funds to individuals or corporations "by subsidy or otherwise"[6]—and taxpayers have standing to challenge giveaways of taxpayer funds. Previously, Arizona courts (like courts in many other states) had not vigorously enforced the gift clause. But in our challenge to the CityNorth subsidy, the Arizona Supreme Court in *Turken v. Gordon*[7] vindicated the intent of the gift clause to prevent corporate subsidies. Although it gave the project at issue a pass because of prior precedents it considered confusing, the Court held that henceforth it would prohibit payments of public funds unless the recipient guarantees roughly proportionate direct and tangible benefits in return.[8]

It is also important to recognize that state constitutions are not necessarily finished documents. Especially at a time of expanding encroachments on individual liberty, state constitutions can be amended not only to prevent abuses by state and local governments but also to erect a federalism shield against excesses by the national government. In 2002, Arizona voters passed two amendments to the state constitution drafted by the Goldwater Institute to protect individual rights that are threatened by Washington, D.C. Those amendments in turn were adopted in other states. First was the Health Care Freedom Act,[9] which protects the right of Arizonans to choose whether to participate in a health insurance system and to control lawful medical decisions.

The second was the Save Our Secret Ballot Act,[10] which protects the right of workers to determine by secret ballot whether or not to form a union. Both constitutional provisions are under legal attack by the Obama administration.

The foregoing discussion barely scratches the surface in terms of the potential for state constitutions to curb abuses of government power and protect individual freedom. But that potential can be realized only on two conditions: skilled advocates filing the right cases and judges willing to enforce constitutional provisions.

States employ a wide variety of methods for the appointment of judges. Some states have direct elections for judges. Others have a system similar to the federal process, by which the governor appoints judges and the state legislature confirms them. Still others have systems in which independent commissions select potential nominees from which the governor chooses. In some states, judges face retention elections. Some judicial elections are contested; others provide a "yes" or "no" choice. Some contested elections are partisan while others are not. Some judicial appointments are made on the basis of political patronage; others are designed to produce choices based on merit. In some merit-based selection systems, the state bar plays a significant role. Some states have different processes for different courts.

As a result of the multitude of methods, it is difficult to make any generalizations about state judicial selection, except for one: *all* of them provide opportunities for public influence, whether through the political process, the judicial selection process, or both. In particular, where governors are involved in judicial appointments, as they usually are, the election of governors who are committed to sound judicial appointments is crucially important. Similarly, where judges are directly elected or subjected to retention elections, these elections often are among the most significant to appear on the ballot. Yet judicial nominations rarely are an issue in gubernatorial elections; and in most states, though with some noteworthy recent exceptions, judicial elections rarely evoke substantial public interest or participation.

In addition to state constitutional decisions, state judges make most of the decisions that directly impact the lives of ordinary people, from personal injury lawsuits, to property and contract disputes, to family law, to most criminal cases. The identity of state judges therefore is very important. Whether through judicial-election or retention campaigns, electing governors, or participating in a merit-based selection process, it is vitally important for freedom advocates to engage in the selection of state court judges.

NOTES

Chapter 1

1. 83 U.S. 36 (1873).
2. I recount the story of the *Slaughter-House Cases* and their continuing impact on economic liberty in *Death Grip: Loosening the Law's Stranglehold over Economic Liberty* (Hoover Institution Press, 2011).
3. 323 U.S. 214 (1944).
4. Nixon's clumsy and sometimes crude efforts to reshape the Supreme Court are recounted in John W. Dean and Michael Rafkin, *The Rehnquist Choice: The Untold Story of the Nixon Appointment That Redefined the Supreme Court* (Free Press, 2001). Nixon's penchant for recording his own conversations makes this book all the more remarkable and insightful, given that Dean was able to directly present the president's thoughts and often colorful language about possible Court nominees. I am indebted to my friend Barry Goldwater, Jr., for bringing this book to my attention.
5. 410 U.S. 113 (1973).
6. 561 U.S. 3025 (2010).
7. 130 S.Ct. 876 (2010).

8. I would argue that *Bush v. Gore*, 531 U.S. 98 (2000), is one example of where they did, with liberal and conservative justices taking positions opposite what one might have expected given their views in other cases.

9. See Clint Bolick, *David's Hammer: The Case for an Activist Judiciary* (Cato Institute, 2007).

10. See Stephen Breyer, *Active Liberty: Interpreting Our Democratic Constitution* (Alfred A. Knopf, 2005).

11. That was the same year I graduated from law school at the University of California at Davis. I often lament that if the Federalist Society had been established a few years earlier, my generally miserable experience at a very hostile left-wing law school might have been tempered a bit. It is refreshing now to return to my alma mater and find a flourishing Federalist Society chapter there.

12. 505 U.S. 833 (1992).

Chapter 2

1. See Bolick, *David's Hammer*, pp. 35–47.

2. Quoted in Randy E. Barnett, "James Madison's Ninth Amendment," in Barnett, ed., *The Rights Retained by the People* (George Mason University Press, 1989), p. 21.

3. For an insightful analysis of this presumption and argument for why it is wrong, see Randy E. Barnett, *Restoring the Lost Constitution: The Presumption of Liberty* (Princeton University Press, 2004).

4. 347 U.S. 483 (1954).

Chapter 3

1. This fascinating story is recounted in Cliff Sloan and David McKean, *The Great Decision: Jefferson, Marshall, and the Battle for the Supreme Court* (PublicAffairs, 2009).

2. *Marbury v. Madison*, 5 U.S. 137 (1803).

3. 32 U.S. 243 (1833).

4. 60 U.S. 663 (1857).

5. To put it mildly, we have lost sight of that original understanding of civil rights, turning the concept from equality of opportunity into equality of results, and from individual liberty into group entitlements. The results have been divisive and tragic. I have addressed that topic in several books, most recently *The Affirmative Action Fraud: Can We Restore the American Civil Rights Vision?* (Cato Institute, 1996).

6. Many of the congressional debates during that period centered around whether Congress possessed constitutional authority to accomplish the desired objectives. Such concerns have all but disappeared from congressional debate, with recent examples including President George W. Bush signing federal campaign finance restrictions whose constitutionality he openly questioned and then House speaker Nancy Pelosi scoffing at concerns about the constitutionality of the sweeping federal health insurance law. The abandonment of any measure of executive and legislative self-restraint amplifies the importance of judicial review.

7. I discuss the purposes of the privileges or immunities clause, its obliteration in the *Slaughter-House Cases*, and the tragic consequences of that decision in my most recent book, *Death Grip*.

8. 83 U.S. 130 (1873).

9. 92 U.S. 542 (1875).

10. 163 U.S. 537 (1896).

11. 118 U.S. 356 (1886).

12. 198 U.S. 45 (1905).

13. 268 U.S. 510 (1925).

14. 290 U.S. 398 (1934).

15. 304 U.S. 144 (1938).

16. 295 U.S. 495 (1935).

17. 317 U.S. 111 (1942).

18. 319 U.S. 624 (1943).

19. 323 U.S. 214 (1944).

20. 347 U.S. 483 (1954).

21. 394 U.S. 557 (1969).

22. 406 U.S. 205 (1972). Although this case occurred during the Nixon administration, liberals still were firmly in control of the Court until well into the Reagan administration.

23. *Virginia State Board of Pharmacy v. Virginia Citizens Consumer Council, Inc.*, 425 U.S. 748 (1976).

24. 384 U.S. 436 (1966).

25. 397 U.S. 254 (1970).

26. *Swann v. Charlotte-Mecklenburg Board of Education*, 402 U.S. 1 (1970).

27. 410 U.S. 113 (1973).

Chapter 4

1. Regnery Publishing, Inc., 2005.

2. Basic Books, 2005.

3. Paul Gewirtz and Chad Golder, "So Who Are the Activists?" *New York Times* (July 6, 2005), p. A23.

4. See Bolick, *David's Hammer*, pp. 29–30.

5. *Id.*, pp. 87–96.

6. 530 U.S. 57 (2000).

7. *Granholm v. Heald*, 544 U.S. 460 (2005). The decision is proof of the unique potential for wine to bring together unusual bedfellows.

8. *Nollan v. California Coastal Commission*, 483 U.S. 825 (1987).

9. *Lucas v. South Carolina Coastal Council*, 505 U.S. 1003 (1992).

10. 512 U.S. 374 (1994).

11. 545 U.S. 469 (2005).

12. I refer to his decision as "inexplicable" given his votes in the earlier property rights cases and his recognition in a case involving the often-pernicious government practice of civil asset forfeiture of the "essential principle" that "[i]ndividual freedom finds tangible expression in property rights." *United States v. James Daniel Good Real Property*, 510 U.S. 43, 61 (1993).

13. After the neighborhood was demolished, Pfizer decided to move out of New London.

14. *Regents of the University of California v. Bakke*, 438 U.S. 265 (1978).

15. *Wygant v. Jackson Board of Education*, 476 U.S. 267 (1986).

16. 488 U.S. 469 (1989).

17. 515 U.S. 200 (1995).

18. 539 U.S. 244 (2003).

19. 539 U.S. 306 (2003).

20. I am proud to have helped lead the nationwide legal defense of school choice. Those efforts are recounted in Clint Bolick, *Voucher Wars: Waging the Legal Battle Over School Choice* (Cato Institute, 2003). Although the federal constitutional battle has been won, at least for now, it continues to be fought under state constitutions, as I will describe in the concluding section.

21. *Committee for Public Education v. Nyquist*, 413 U.S. 756 (1973).

22. *Mueller v. Allen*, 463 U.S. 388 (1983).

23. 536 U.S. 639 (2002).

24. 554 U.S. 570 (2008).

25. 561 U.S. 3025 (2010).

26. 424 U.S. 1 (1976).

27. 540 U.S. 93 (2003).

28. 548 U.S. 230 (2006).

29. 130 S.Ct. 876 (2010).

30. *Arizona Free Enterprise Club's Freedom Club PAC v. Bennett*, 131 S.Ct. 2806 (2011).

31. 514 U.S. 549 (1995).

32. 529 U.S. 598 (2000).

33. 545 U.S. 1 (2005).

34. 546 U.S. 243 (2006).

35. 129 S.Ct. 2579 (2009).

36. *Northwest Austin Municipal Utility District No. 1 v. Holder*, 129 S.Ct. 2504 (2009).

37. Arizona, which should never have been encompassed within section 5 to begin with and which is ineligible to bail out from its requirements, subsequently has challenged the constitutionality of section 5.

38. 131 S.Ct. 1968 (2011).
39. 131 S.Ct. 455 (2010).

Postscript

1. William J. Brennan Jr., "State Constitutions and the Protection of Individual Rights," *Harvard Law Review*, vol. 90, p. 489 (1977); and "The Bill of Rights and the States: The Revival of State Constitutions as Guardians of Individual Rights," *New York University Law Review*, vol. 61, p. 535 (1986).

2. *San Antonio Independent School District v. Rodriguez*, 411 U.S. 1 (1973).

3. See Marc Lacey, "A Watchdog for Conservative Ideals," *New York Times* (Dec. 26, 2011), p. A10.

4. Arizona Constitution article II, section 7.

5. *Bailey v. Myers*, 76 P.3d 898 (Ariz. App. 2003).

6. Arizona Constitution article IX, section 7.

7. 224 P.3d 158 (Ariz. 2010).

8. As is so often the case, government planners could not overcome market forces, and the poorly conceived CityNorth project ended up filing for bankruptcy.

9. Arizona Constitution article XXVII, section 2.

10. Arizona Constitution article II, section 37.

ABOUT THE AUTHOR

Clint Bolick is one of America's premier constitutional litigators, having won U.S. Supreme Court decisions on school vouchers and the direct interstate shipment of wine to consumers and numerous other precedent-setting cases in federal and state courts around the nation. In a recent profile, the *New York Times* said that Bolick is "known for his aggressive litigation to defend individual liberties." *Legal Times* named him one of the ninety greatest DC lawyers of the past thirty years; *American Lawyer* named him one of three lawyers of the year in 2003; and he received the Bradley Prize in 2006. Bolick, who heads the Goldwater Institute's Scharf-Norton Center for Constitutional Litigation in Phoenix, also serves as a research fellow at the Hoover Institution. He is the author of several books, most recently *Death Grip: Loosening the Law's Stranglehold over Economic Liberty* (2011) and *David's Hammer: The Case for an Activist Judiciary* (2007).

INDEX

Other Books by Clint Bolick

NONFICTION

Death Grip: Loosening the Law's Stranglehold
Over Economic Liberty (2011)*

David's Hammer: The Case for an Activist Judiciary (2007)

Leviathan: The Growth of Local Government and
the Erosion of Liberty (2004)*

Voucher Wars: Waging the Legal Battle Over School Choice (2003)

Transformation: The Promise and Politics of Empowerment (1998)

The Affirmative Action Fraud: Can We Restore
the American Civil Rights Vision? (1996)

Unfinished Business: A Civil Rights Strategy
for America's Third Century (1990)

Changing Course: Civil Rights at the Crossroads (1988)

FICTION

Nicki's Girl (2007)

*Published by Hoover Institution Press.